1, 2, & 3 John

THE

CROSSWAY CLASSIC

COMMENTARIES

1, 2, & 3 John

JOHN CALVIN & MATTHEW HENRY

SERIES EDITORS

ALISTER MCGRATH

J. I. PACKER

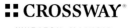

:: CROSSWAY®

WHEATON, ILLINOIS

Cover design: Jordan Singer

First printing, 1998

Printed in the United States of America

Library of Congress Cataloging-in-Publication Data
Calvin, Jean, 1509–1564.
 1, 2, & 3 John / by John Calvin, Matthew Henry.
  p. cm. — (The Crossway classic commentaries)
 ISBN 13: 978-0-89107-993-4
 ISBN 10: 0-89107-993-9
 1. Bible. N.T. Epistles of John—Commentaries. I. Henry
Matthew, 1662–1714. II. Title. III. Series.
BS2805.3.C35   1998
227'.94077—dc21   99-11104

Crossway is a publishing ministry of Good News Publishers.

CH 24 23 22 21 20 19 18 17 16

First British edition 1998

Production and Printing in the United States of America for

CROSSWAY

Norton Street, Nottingham, England NG7 3HR

ISBN 1-85684-162-6

Contents

Series Preface

The purpose of the Crossway Classic Commentaries is to make some of the most valuable commentaries on the books of the Bible, by some of the greatest Bible teachers and theologians in the last five hundred years, available to a new generation. These books will help today's readers learn truth, wisdom, and devotion from such authors as J. C. Ryle, Martin Luther, John Calvin, J. B. Lightfoot, John Owen, Charles Spurgeon, Charles Hodge, and Matthew Henry.

We do not apologize for the age of some of the items chosen. In the realm of practical exposition promoting godliness, the old is often better than the new. Spiritual vision and authority, based on an accurate handling of the biblical text, are the qualities that have been primarily sought in deciding what to include.

So far as is possible, everything is tailored to the needs and enrichment of thoughtful readers—lay Christians, students, and those in the ministry. The originals, some of which were written at a high technical level, have been abridged as needed, simplified stylistically, and unburdened of foreign words. However, the intention of this series is never to change any thoughts of the original authors, but to faithfully convey them in an understandable fashion.

The publishers are grateful to Dr. Alister McGrath of Wycliffe Hall, Oxford, Dr. J. I. Packer of Regent College, Vancouver, and Watermark of Norfolk, England, for the work of selecting and editing that now brings this project to fruition.

THE PUBLISHERS
Crossway Books
Wheaton, Illinois

Introduction

The first letter of John was written to churches that had been plagued and split by the teaching known as Gnosticism. Formed from the Greek word for knowledge (gnosis), that term points to the Gnostic claim to have vital knowledge that ordinary Christians lacked. Gnosticism was the liberalism, modernism, and New-Age syncretism of the apostolic era. Like its present-day counterparts, it actually sought to destroy Christianity by attempting to update and reshape it in light of the supposed certainties of secular learning. It started from the conviction that the material order, including the human body, is worthless, contemptible, and indeed evil, and that mankind's basic religious problem is not, as Jews and Christians thought, moral (our sin, producing guilt before God), but physical (imprisonment in our bodies, producing isolation from God). Accordingly, it viewed the teaching—doctrinal, ethical, and devotional—that the apostles gave in their evangelistic and pastoral ministries as crude and misconceived. It rejected the Incarnation and Atonement, reimagined Jesus as an inspired teacher of secret knowledge about spiritual powers, ascetic routines, and mystical moments, and called on believers to qualify as God's elite by embracing this revised version of their faith. Proud, self-satisfied, and sure they were right, the Gnostics disrupted churches, to the point of walking out on those who held fast to the apostolic message.

John wrote this letter to stabilize some of the victims of this treatment, and that is the angle of approach that present-day expositors usually pursue. Nor is there anything wrong with so doing; on the contrary, it is important to get clear on what John was up against, so that we can trace out the ad hominem pastoral logic of the letter and see why John says what he says in the order and manner in which he says it. Calvin's procedure in his commentary on 1 John, however, is different, and complementary to what I have described—though (let me say at once) no less valuable for that.

What does Calvin do? He projects the letter as a proclamation of God's love in Jesus Christ, his incarnate Son and Word of life, and of the transformed existence of believers. He treats it as truth for Christians in every age, starting with his own. He highlights incarnation, redemption, regeneration, and adoption as the central realities of God's saving work; he presents obedient love to God and self-denying, Christlike love to fellow saints as the central realities of Christian behavior; and he points to fellowship with the Father and the Son through the Spirit, with inward peace and a sure hope of glory as the central realities of Christian existence. And, bypassing the details of early-church Gnosticism as not so relevant for his readers, he mounts a corrective polemic against Roman Catholic ideas that work against full knowledge of God's grace. Practical relevance for head and heart is what he seeks throughout—and what he finds.

Calvin never commented on 2 and 3 John. So this Crossway Classic volume is rounded off with the exposition of both in the great *Commentary of Matthew Henry* (1662-1714). Though all the material after Acts was put into shape by others following Henry's death, it is likely that Henry left them something to work on, and the comments on these two small letters are very much in Henry's style. Henry and his continuators inherited more than a century and a half of exact exegesis stemming from the Reformation plus a wealth of applicatory reflection in the treatises of Puritan writers, and, drawing on these riches, they worked to standards of analysis and practicality that have secured for their work a permanent place on the bookshelves of serious preachers and Bible students. Henry on 2 and 3 John complements Calvin on 1 John in a fully worthy way, as readers will quickly discover.

J. I. Packer

1 John
by John Calvin

Preface
to 1 John

This letter is altogether worthy of the spirit of that disciple who, above others, was loved by Christ so that he might exhibit Christ as a friend to us. But it contains doctrines mixed with exhortations, for John speaks of the eternal deity of Christ, and at the same time of the incomparable grace that Christ brought with him when he appeared in the world, and generally of all his blessings; John especially commends and extols the inestimable grace of divine adoption.

He grounds his exhortations on these truths; and at one time he admonishes us generally to lead a pious and holy life, and at another time he expressly enjoins love. But he does none of these things in a regular order, for he mixes teaching with exhortation everywhere. But he particularly urges brotherly love; he also touches on other things, such as the need to beware of impostors, and similar things. But each detail will be dealt with in its own place.

Chapter 1

1-2. That which was from the beginning, which we have heard, which we have seen with our eyes, which we have looked at and our hands have touched—this we proclaim concerning the Word of life. The life appeared; we have seen it and testify to it, and we proclaim to you the eternal life, which was with the Father and has appeared to us.

First, he shows that **life** has been exhibited to us in Christ, which, as it is an incomparable good, ought to rouse and inflame all our power with a wonderful desire for it, and with love of it. It is said, in a few plain words, that life **appeared**; but if we consider what a miserable and horrible condition death is, and also what the kingdom and the glory of immortality is, we shall perceive that there is something here more magnificent than can be expressed in any words.

The apostle's object in setting before us the vast good, indeed the chief and only true happiness that God has conferred on us in his own Son, is to raise our thoughts above; but as the greatness of the subject requires the truth to be certain and fully proved, it is much dwelt on here. For these words—**That which . . . we have heard, which we have seen with our eyes, which we have looked at**—serve to strengthen our faith in the Gospel. Indeed, it is not without reason that the apostle makes so many strong assertions, for since our salvation depends on the Gospel, its certainty is in the highest degree necessary; and how difficult it is for us to believe, each one of us knows too well by his own experience. To believe is not lightly to form an opinion, or to assent only to what is said; rather, it is a firm, undoubting conviction, so that we may dare to subscribe to the truth as fully proved. It is for this reason that the apostle heaps together so many things in confirmation of the Gospel.

1. That which was from the beginning. As the passage is abrupt and involved, the words may be rearranged in order to make the sense clearer: "We announce to you the Word of life, which was from the beginning and was truly testified to us in all manner of ways—namely, that life has appeared in him." Or if you prefer, the meaning may be given thus: "What we announce to you respecting the Word of life has been from the beginning and has been openly shown to us: life appeared in him." But the words **That which was from the beginning** doubtless refer to the divinity of Christ, for God did not appear in the flesh from the beginning; but he who always was life and the eternal Word of God appeared in the fullness of time as man. Again, what follows about looking at and touching with the hands refers to his human nature. But as the two natures constitute only one person, and Christ is one—he came from the Father that he might put on our flesh—the apostle rightly declares that he is the same; he had been invisible and afterwards became visible.

This disproves Servetus' senseless argument that the nature and essence of deity became one with the flesh, and that thus the Word was transformed into flesh because the life-giving Word was seen in the flesh.

Let us then bear in mind that this doctrine of the Gospel is declared here: he who in the flesh really proved himself to be the Son of God, and was acknowledged to be the Son of God, was always God's invisible Word, for John is not here referring to the beginning of the world, but ascends much higher.

Which we have heard, which we have seen. This was not merely hearing a report (to which little credit is usually given), but John means that he had faithfully learned from his Master those things that he taught, so that he alleged nothing thoughtlessly and rashly. And, doubtless, no one is a fit teacher in the church who has not been a disciple of the Son of God and rightly instructed in his school, since his authority alone ought to prevail.

With our eyes. This is no redundancy, but a fuller expression for the sake of amplifying. John was not satisfied with merely seeing, but added, **which we have looked at and our hands have touched.** By these words he shows that he taught nothing but what had been really made known to him.

It may seem, however, that the evidence of the senses availed little on the present subject, for the power of Christ could not be perceived by the eyes or felt by the hands. To this I answer that the same thing is said here as in John 1:14: "We have seen his glory, the glory of the one and only Son," for he was not known as the Son of God by the external form of his body, but because he gave clear proofs of his divine power, so that the majesty of the Father shone in him as in a living and distinct image. As the words in 1 John are in the plural, and the subject applies equally to all the apostles, I am disposed to include them, especially as the authority of testimony is what is under discussion.

But Servetus' wickedness (as I have said before) is as frivolous as it is impudent when he argues that these words prove that the Word of God became visible and capable of being handled; he either impiously destroys or mingles together the twofold nature of Christ. This is, therefore, a pure figment. When he denies Christ's humanity, he wholly takes away the reality of his human nature and at the same time denies that Christ is called the Son of God for any other reason than that he was conceived by the power of the Holy Spirit. Servetus takes away Christ's own subsistence in God. Hence it follows that he was neither God nor man, though he seems to form a confused mass from both. But as the apostle's meaning is evident to us, let us pass by that unprincipled Servetus.

Concerning the Word of life. The genitive here is used adjectivally— "vivifying" or "life-giving," for in him, as it says in the first chapter of John's Gospel, was life. At the same time, this distinction belongs to the Son of God on two accounts: because he has infused life into all creatures, and because he now restores life to us when we had perished, having been extinguished by Adam's sin. Moreover, the term **Word** may be explained in two ways—either of Christ, or of the gospel teaching, which is how salvation is brought to us. But as its substance is Christ, and as it contains nothing other than the fact that he, who had always been with the Father, at length appeared to us, the first view seems to me the simpler and more genuine. Moreover, it appears more fully from the Gospel that the wisdom that lives in God is called the Word.

2. The life appeared. It is as though he had said, "We testify of the life-giving Word, for life has appeared." The sense may at the same time be a double one: that Christ, who is life and the fountain of life, has appeared, or that life has been openly offered to us in Christ. The latter, indeed, necessarily follows from the former. Yet as for the meaning, the two things differ, like cause and effect. When he repeats, **we proclaim** or announce **to you the eternal life,** he is speaking, I have no doubt, about the effect—he announces that life is obtained for us in Christ.

From this we learn that when Christ is preached to us, the kingdom of heaven is opened to us, so that being raised from death we may live the life of God.

Which was with the Father. This is true not only from the time when the world was formed, but also from eternity, for he was always God, the fountain of life; and the power and the faculty of vivifying was possessed by his eternal wisdom. But he did not actually exercise it before the creation of the world, and from the time when God began to exhibit the Word, that power which before had been hidden diffused itself over all created things. Some manifestation had already been made; so the apostle had something else in view—that is, that life at last appeared in Christ when he in our flesh completed the work of redemption. Though even under the law the fathers were associates and partakers of the same life, yet we know that they were shut up under the hope that was to be revealed. It was necessary for them to seek life from the death and resurrection of Christ; but the event was not only far remote from their eyes, but also hidden from their minds. They depended, then, on the hope of revelation, which at last in due time followed. They could not, indeed, have obtained life unless it appeared to them in some way; but the difference between us and them is that we hold him already revealed as it were in our hands, whereas when they sought him he was promised to them obscurely in types.

But the apostle's object is to remove the idea of novelty, which might have lessened the dignity of the Gospel. He therefore says that life had not now at last begun to be, though it had only recently appeared, for it was always with the Father.

3-7. We proclaim to you what we have seen and heard, so that you also may have fellowship with us. And our fellowship is with the Father and with his Son, Jesus Christ. We write this to make our joy complete. This is the message we have heard from him and declare to you: God is light; in him there is no darkness at all. If we claim to have fellowship with him yet walk in the darkness, we lie and do not live by the truth. But if we walk in the light, as he is in the light, we have fellowship with one another, and the blood of Jesus, his Son, purifies us from every sin.

3. What we have seen. John now repeats the words **seen** and **heard** for the third and second time, so that nothing might be lacking as to the real certainty of his doctrine. It ought to be carefully noticed that the heralds of the Gospel chosen by Christ were those who were fit and faithful witnesses of all those things that they were to declare. He also testifies of the feeling of their heart, for he says that he was moved to write by no other reason than to invite those to whom he was writing to participate in an inestimable good. Hence it appears how much care he had for their salvation; and this served not a little to induce them to believe, for we must be extremely ungrateful if we refuse to listen to someone who wishes to communicate to us a part of the happiness that he has obtained.

John also sets out the fruit received from the Gospel—namely, that we are united to God by it, and to his Son Christ, in whom is found the chief good. It was necessary for him to add this second clause, not only so that he might show the gospel doctrine as precious and lovely, but also so he might show that he wished them to be his associates for no other reason but to lead them to God, so that they might all be one in God. For the ungodly also have a mutual union between themselves, but it is without God; indeed, it alienates them more and more from God, and that is the extreme of all evils. Indeed, as has been stated, our only true happiness is to be received into God's favor, so that we may be really united to him in Christ. John speaks about this in the seventeenth chapter of his Gospel.

In short, John declares that as the apostles were adopted by Christ as brothers, being gathered into one body so they might be united together with God, so also Christ does with other colleagues. Though they are many, they are made partakers of this holy and blessed union.

4. To make our joy complete. By complete joy the apostle expresses more clearly the complete and perfect happiness that we obtain through the Gospel; at the same time he reminds the faithful where they ought to fix all their affections. How true it is that "where your treasure is, there your heart will be also" (Matthew 6:21)! So, whoever really perceives what fellowship with God is will be satisfied with it alone and will no more burn with desires for other things. "LORD," says David, "you have assigned me my portion and my cup; you have made my lot secure. The boundary lines have fallen for me in pleasant places" (Psalm 16:5-6). Similarly, Paul declares that he considered everything "rubbish" in comparison with Christ alone (Philippians 3:8). Therefore, those who have become proficient in the Gospel are those who think themselves happy to have communion with God and are satisfied only with that, so that they prefer it to the whole world and are ready for its sake to relinquish everything else.

5. This is the message or promise. I do not disapprove of the old interpretation, "This is the announcement" or message. The Greek word used here usually means a promise, but John is speaking here about the aforementioned testimony generally, and the context seems to require the other meaning, unless you give this explanation: "The promise that we bring to you includes this or has this condition attached to it." Thus the apostle's meaning would be clear to us. For his object here was not to include the whole doctrine of the Gospel but to show that if we desire to enjoy Christ and his blessings, we have to be conformed to God in righteousness and holiness. Paul says the same thing in Titus 2:11-12: "The grace of God that brings salvation has appeared to all men. It teaches us to say 'No' to ungodliness and worldly passions, and to live self-controlled, upright and godly lives in this present age," except that here John says metaphorically that **we are to walk in the light** because **God is light**.

Though he calls God **light** and says that he is **in the light**, such expressions are not to be taken too strictly. Why Satan is called the prince of darkness is clear enough. When, therefore, God on the other hand is called the Father of light, and also **light**, we first understand that there is nothing in him but what is bright, pure, and unalloyed, and, second, that he makes all things so clear by his brightness that he allows nothing vicious or perverted, no spots or filth, no hypocrisy or fraud, to remain hidden. So the sum of it all is that since there is no union between light and darkness, there is a separation between us and God as long as we walk in darkness; the fellowship that John mentions cannot exist unless we also become pure and holy.

In him there is no darkness at all. This manner of speaking is commonly used by John to amplify what he has affirmed by a negative. The meaning, then, is that God is such a light that no darkness belongs to him. Hence it follows that he hates an evil conscience, pollution, wickedness, and everything that pertains to darkness.

6. If we claim. It is indeed an argument from what is inconsistent when he concludes that people who walk in darkness are alienated from God. This doctrine, however, depends on a higher principle: God sanctifies all who are his. It is not a mere precept that John gives here, requiring that our life should be holy; rather, he shows that the grace of Christ serves to dissipate darkness and to kindle in us the light of God, as though he said, "What God communicates to us is not a vain fiction, for it is necessary that the power and effect of this fellowship shine in our life; otherwise the possession of the Gospel is fallacious." What he adds—and **do not live by the truth**—is the same as saying, "We do not act truthfully; we do not regard what is true and right." This manner of speaking, as I have observed before, is frequently used by John.

7. But if we walk in the light. He now says that the proof of our union with God is certain if we conform to him; not that purity of life conciliates us to God, as the prior cause. Rather, the apostle means that our union with God is made evident by the effect—that is, when his purity shines in us. And doubtless this is a fact. Wherever God comes, all things are so imbued with his holiness that he washes away all filth; for without him we have nothing but corruption and darkness. Hence it is evident that no one leads a holy life unless he is united to God.

In saying **we have fellowship with one another**, he is not speaking simply about human beings. He is setting God on one side and us on the other.

However, it may be asked, "What human beings can so exhibit God's light in their life that this likeness that John requires should exist? For it would then be necessary to be wholly pure and free from darkness." To this I answer that expressions of this kind are accommodated to human capacity, so that a person is said to be like God if he aspires to his likeness, however distant from it he may as yet be. The example should not be applied in any other way than according to this passage. People who walk in the darkness are those who are not ruled by the fear of God and who do not, with a pure conscience, devote themselves wholly to God and seek to promote his glory. On the other hand, people who spend their lives—every part of them—in the fear and service of God with sincerity of heart and who faithfully worship him walk in the light, for they keep to the right way, though they may offend in many things and sigh under the burden of the flesh. So then, integrity of conscience distinguishes light from darkness.

And the blood of Jesus. After teaching what is the bond of our union with God, John now shows what fruit comes from it—namely, our sins are freely forgiven. This is the blessedness that David describes in Psalm 32 in order that we may know that we are most miserable until, being renewed by God's Spirit, we serve him with a sincere heart. For who can be imagined more miserable than a person whom God hates and abominates, and over whose head is suspended both the wrath of God and eternal death?

This passage is remarkable; from it we learn, first, that the expiation of Christ, effected by his death, really belongs to us when we do what is right and just, in uprightness of heart; for Christ is no redeemer except to those who turn from iniquity and lead a new life. If, then, we desire to have God propitious to us, so as to forgive our sins, we ought not to forgive ourselves. In short, remission of sins cannot be separated from repentance; nor can the peace of God be in those hearts where the fear of God does not prevail.

Second, this passage shows that the free pardon of sins is given us not just once, but is a benefit that always remains in the church and is offered to the faithful every day. For the apostle is writing to the faithful here, as doubtless no one has ever been, nor ever will be, who can please God in any other way, since all are guilty before him; for however strong a desire there may be in us to act rightly, we always go to God hesitatingly. Yet what is half done obtains no approval from God. In the meantime, by new sins we continually separate ourselves, as far as we can, from the grace of God. Thus it is that all the saints need daily forgiveness of sins, for this alone keeps us in the family of God.

By saying **from every [margin, "all"] sin** John implies that we are, on many accounts, guilty before God, so that doubtless there is no one who does not have many vices. But he shows that no sins prevent the godly, and those who fear God, from obtaining his favor. He also points out the way in which we can obtain pardon, and also the ground of our cleansing: Christ expiated our sins by his blood. John says that all godly people unquestionably share in this cleansing.

The whole of his doctrine has been wickedly perverted by the Sophists, who imagine that pardon of sins is given us, as it were, in baptism. They maintain that Christ's blood is only of any avail in baptism, and they teach that after baptism God is reconciled only by satisfactions. Indeed, they leave some part to the blood of Christ; but when they assign merit to works, even in the least degree, they wholly subvert what John teaches here about the way of expiating sins and of being reconciled to God. For these two things—being cleansed by the blood of Christ and being cleansed by works—can never be harmonized, for John assigns the whole of it, not just half of it, to the blood of Christ.

So then, the sum of what he says is that the faithful know with certainty that they are accepted by God, because he has been reconciled to them through the sacrifice of the death of Christ. A sacrifice must include cleansing and satisfaction. Hence the power and efficacy of these belong to the blood of Christ alone.

In this way the idea of indulgences is disproved, for they add the blood and merits of martyrs as though the blood of Christ were not sufficient. If this doctrine stands, the blood of Christ does not cleanse us but comes in, as it were, as a partial aid. Thus consciences are held in suspense, whereas the apostle tells us to rely on the blood of Christ.

8-10. If we claim to be without sin, we deceive ourselves and the truth is not in us. If we confess our sins, he is faithful and just and will forgive us our sins and purify us from all unrighteousness. If we claim we have not sinned, we make him out to be a liar and his word has no place in our lives.

8. If we claim. He now commends grace from its necessity; for as no one is free from sin, he is saying that we are all lost and undone unless the Lord comes to our aid with the remedy of pardon. The reason he dwells so much on the fact that no one is innocent is so that everyone may now fully know they stand in need of mercy to deliver them from punishment, and that they may thus be roused to seek the necessary blessing.

By the word **sin** here is meant not only corrupt and vicious inclination, but the fault or sinful act that renders us guilty before God. As this is a universal declaration, it follows that none of the saints, past, present or future, are exempt from the number. Hence it was quite right of Augustine to refute the Pelagians' argument by adducing this passage against them. He wisely thought that the confession of guilt is not required to humble us but lest we should deceive ourselves by lying.

And the truth is not in us. In adding this, he is confirming the previous sentence (**we deceive ourselves**) in his usual way, by repeating it with other words—though it is not a simple repetition, as elsewhere, but rather he is saying that people are deceived if they glory in falsehood.

9. If we confess. Again he promises to the faithful that God will be propitious to them, provided they acknowledge themselves to be sinners. It is important to be fully persuaded that when we have sinned, there is a reconciliation with God ready and prepared for us; otherwise we shall always be carrying hell within us. Indeed, few people consider how miserable and wretched a doubting conscience is; but the truth is that hell reigns where there is no peace with God. So it becomes all the more important to receive with our whole hearts this promise that offers free pardon to all who confess their sins. Moreover, this is based on God's justice, because God who promises is true and just. Those who think that he is called **just** because he justifies us freely are being too refined, I think; for justice or righteousness here depends on faithfulness, and both are attached to the promise. God might have been just if he dealt with us with all the rigor of justice; but as he has bound himself to us by his Word, he would not have himself deemed just unless he forgives.

But this confession, as it is made to God, must be in sincerity; since the heart cannot speak to God without newness of life, it includes true repentance. God indeed forgives freely, but in such a way that the facility of mercy does not become an enticement to sin.

And purify us. This verb seems to be taken in a different sense than previously, for in verse 7 John had said that we are purified by the blood of Jesus, but here, having spoken of pardon, he adds that God purifies us from all unrighteousness; this second clause is different from the previous one. Thus he is telling us that a double fruit comes to us from confession—that God, being reconciled by Christ's sacrifice, forgives us and that he renews and reforms us.

If anyone objects that as long as we remain in the world we are never cleansed from all unrighteousness, with regard to our reformation this is indeed true; but John is not referring to what God now performs in us. He is faithful, he says, and will purify us, but not completely today or tomorrow; for as long as we are surrounded with flesh, we ought to be in a continual state of progress. But what God has begun, he goes on to do every day, until at last he completes it. So Paul says that we are chosen to appear without blame before God (Colossians 1:22); and in another passage he says that the church is cleansed, that it might be "without stain or wrinkle" (Ephesians 5:27).

If anyone prefers another explanation—that the apostle is saying the same things twice over—I will not object.

10. We make him out to be a liar. John goes still further, saying that those who claim purity for themselves blaspheme God. We see that he everywhere represents the whole human race as guilty of sin.

Whoever tries to escape this charge, then, carries on war with God and accuses him of falsehood, as though he condemned people who did not deserve it. To confirm this, John adds, **and his word has no place in our lives,** by which he is saying that we reject this great truth that everyone is guilty.

Thus we learn that we only make due progress in the knowledge of the Word of the Lord when we become really humbled and groan under the burden of our sins and learn to flee to God's mercy and find rest in nothing except his fatherly favor.

Chapter 2

1-2. My dear children, I write this to you so that you will not sin. But if anybody does sin, we have one who speaks to the Father in our defense— Jesus Christ, the Righteous One. He is the atoning sacrifice for our sins, and not only for ours but also for the sins of the whole world.

1. My dear children. It is not only the sum and substance of the preceding doctrine, but the meaning of almost the whole Gospel, that we are to depart from sin; and yet, though we are always exposed to God's judgment, we are certain that Christ so intercedes by the sacrifice of his death that the Father is propitious to us. In the meantime, John also anticipates an objection, lest anyone should think that he gave license to sin when he spoke of God's mercy and showed that it is presented to us all. So he joins together two parts of the Gospel, which unreasonable people separate and thus lacerate and mutilate. Besides, the doctrine of grace has always been maligned by the ungodly. When the expiation of sins by Christ is displayed, they boastingly say that a license is thus given to sin.

To obviate these malicious misrepresentations, the apostle testifies first that the aim of his teaching was to keep people from sinning; for when he says **so that you will not sin,** he simply means that we should abstain from sins as far as human weakness allows. And the same purpose is served by what I have already said respecting fellowship with God: we are to conform to him. However, John is not silent about the free forgiveness of sins; for even if everything else should be confounded, this part of truth ought never to be omitted. On the contrary, what Christ is ought to be preached clearly and distinctly.

So ought we also to do today. As the flesh is inclined to wantonness, people ought to be carefully warned that righteousness and salvation are provided in Christ so that we may become the holy possession of God. Yet whenever it happens that people wantonly abuse God's mercy, there are many surly people who load us with malicious accusations as though we gave loose rein to vices. We ought still boldly to go on and proclaim the grace of Christ, in which especially God's glory shines, and in which consists the whole of our salvation. These barkings of the ungodly ought, I repeat, to be wholly disregarded, for we see that the apostles were also assailed by these attacks.

For this reason the apostle immediately adds the second clause: when we sin **we have one who speaks to the Father in our defense**. By these words he confirms what we have already said, that we are very far from being perfectly righteous, and indeed contract new guilt every day, but that there is still a remedy that can reconcile us to God if we flee to Christ. This alone is what consciences can acquiesce in; it includes our righteousness, and the hope of salvation is based on it.

The conditional particle **if** should be viewed as causal, for it cannot be but that we sin. In short, John means not only that we are called away from sin by the Gospel, because God invites us to himself and offers us the Spirit of regeneration, but also that a provision is made for miserable sinners, so that God will always be propitious toward them, and so the sins by which they are entangled do not prevent them from becoming just, because they have a Mediator to reconcile them to God. But in order to show how we return into favor with God, the apostle says that Christ is our advocate; for he appears before God for this purpose, that he may exercise toward us the power and efficacy of his sacrifice. So that this may be understood better, I will put it more clearly: Christ's intercession is a continual application of his death for our salvation. God's not imputing our sins to us, then, happens because he has regard for Christ as intercessor.

John calls Christ **the Righteous One** and an **atoning sacrifice**. It is necessary for him to be both, so that he might sustain the office and person of an Advocate; for what sinner could reconcile God to us? We are excluded from access to God because no one is pure and free from sin. Hence no one is fit to be a high priest unless he is innocent and separated from sinners, as

Hebrew 7:26 declares. **Atoning sacrifice** is added because no one is fit to be a high priest without a sacrifice. Hence under the law no priest entered the sanctuary without blood; and a sacrifice accompanied prayers as the usual seal, just as God had appointed. By this symbol God meant to show that whoever obtains favor for us must be furnished with a sacrifice; for when God is offended, in order to pacify him a satisfaction is required. Hence it follows that all the saints who have ever been, and who will be in the future, need an Advocate, and no one except Christ is equal to undertake this office. Doubtless John ascribed these two things to Christ in order to show that he is the only true Advocate.

No small consolation comes to us when we hear that Christ not only died for us, to reconcile us to the Father, but that he continually intercedes for us, so that an access in his name is open to us, so that our prayers may be heard. We ought especially, then, beware lest this honor, which belongs uniquely to him, should be transferred to someone else.

But we know that among the Roman Catholics this office is ascribed indiscriminately to the saints. They may not deny that Christ excels others, but they join with him a vast number of associates. Yet these words of Scripture clearly mean that no one who is not a priest can speak to the Father in our defense, and that the priesthood belongs to nobody except Christ. This is not to detract from the intercessions that believers offer for one another in love, but this has nothing to do with the dead, who no longer have dealings with the living, and nothing to do with that patronage that some feign for themselves, that they may not be dependent on Christ alone. Though believers pray for each other, they all, without exception, look to one person who speaks to the Father in their defense.

We must also notice, by the way, that people who imagine that Christ falls on his knees before the Father to pray for us are in gross error. Such thoughts ought to be renounced, for they detract from the celestial glory of Christ. We should keep to the simple truth that the fruit of his death is always new and perpetual. By his intercession, he renders God propitious to us; he sanctifies our prayers by the odor of his sacrifice and also aids us by pleading for us.

2. Not only for ours. John added this by way of amplification, so that the faithful might be assured that the expiation made by Christ extends to all who by faith embrace the Gospel.

Here it may be asked how **the sins of the whole world** have been expiated. I will ignore the dotings of fanatics who say this means salvation extends to all the reprobate and therefore to Satan himself. Such a monstrous thing deserves no refutation. People who seek to avoid this absurdity have said that Christ suffered sufficiently for the whole world, but efficiently only for the chosen. This solution has commonly prevailed among theologians. Though I admit that what has been said is true, I deny that it suits this passage, for John's purpose was none other than to make this benefit common to the whole church. By the word **whole**, then, he does not mean to include the reprobate, but he means those who would believe as well as those who were then scattered through various parts of the world. For the Gospel makes Christ clear, as it should do, when it is declared to be the only true salvation of the world.

3-6. We know that we have come to know him if we obey his commands. The man who says, "I know him," but does not do what he commands is a liar, and the truth is not in him. But if anyone obeys his word, God's love is truly made complete in him. This is how we know we are in him: Whoever claims to live in him must walk as Jesus did.

3. After dealing with the doctrine of the free forgiveness of sins, John comes to the exhortations that belong to it and that depend on it. And first indeed he reminds us that the knowledge of God, derived from the Gospel, is not ineffectual, but obedience proceeds from it. He then shows what God especially requires from us, what is the chief thing in life—namely, love for God. It is not without reason that the Scripture everywhere repeats what we read here of the living knowledge of God. Nothing is more common in the world than to draw the doctrine of religion into frigid speculations. In this way theology has been adulterated by the Sophists of the Sorbonne, so that not the least spark of true religion brightens their whole theology. And curious people everywhere learn enough from God's Word to be able to prattle for the sake of display. In short, no evil has been more common in all ages than professing God's name vainly.

John, then, takes it for granted that the knowledge of God is efficacious. Hence he concludes that people do not by any means know God if they do not keep his precepts or commands. Plato, though groping in darkness, denied that "the beautiful" that he imagined could be known without filling people with admiration for it; so he says in his *Phaedrus* and in other places. How then is it possible for one to know God and to be moved by no feeling? It does not just come from God's nature that to know him is immediately to love him; the Spirit also, who illuminates our minds, inspires our hearts with a feeling appropriate to our knowledge. At the same time the knowledge of God leads us to fear him and to love him, for we cannot know him as Lord and Father, as he reveals himself, without being dutiful children and obedient servants. In short, the doctrine of the Gospel is a lively mirror in which we contemplate the image of God and are transformed into the same, as Paul teaches us in 2 Corinthians 3:18. Where, therefore, there is no pure conscience, nothing can exist but an empty phantom of knowledge.

If we obey his commands. But, some might assert, there is no one who does God's will in everything; there would thus be no knowledge of God in the world. To this I answer that the apostle is not being at all inconsistent, since he has already shown that all are guilty before God. So he does not mean that those who keep his commandments wholly satisfy the law; no such instance can be found in the world. He refers to those who strive, as much as human weakness allows, to shape their life in conformity to God's will. Whenever Scripture speaks of the righteousness of the faithful, it does not exclude the forgiveness of sins, but on the contrary begins with it.

But we are not to conclude from this that faith rests on works; for though everyone receives a testimony to his faith from his works, it does not follow that it is founded on them, since they are added as an evidence. So then, the certainty of faith depends on the grace of Christ alone; but piety and holiness of life distinguish true faith from that knowledge of God that is fictitious and dead, for the truth is that those who are in Christ, as Paul says, have taken off the old self (Colossians 3:9).

4. The man who says, "I know him." How does John prove that people are liars if they boast that they have faith but have no piety? He proves it by the contrary effect, for he has already said that the knowledge of God is efficacious. God is not known by mere imagination; rather, he reveals himself inwardly to our hearts by the Spirit. Besides, though many hypocrites vainly boast that they have faith, the apostle charges all of them with falsehood, for what he says would be superfluous if people made no false and vain profession of Christianity.

5. But if anyone obeys. The apostle now defines what a true keeping of God's law is—namely, to love God. This passage is, I think, incorrectly explained by those who understand that people please the true God if they keep his Word. Rather, take this as its meaning: "to love God in sincerity of heart is to keep his commandments." As I have reminded you already, John was trying to show briefly what God requires from us and what constitutes the holiness of the faithful. Moses said the same thing when he summed up the law: "And now, O Israel, what does the LORD your God ask of you but to fear the LORD your God, to walk in all his ways, to love him . . . ?" (Deuteronomy 10:12). And again he says, "Choose life . . . that you may love the LORD your God, listen to his voice, and hold fast to him" (Deuteronomy 30:19-20). The law, which is spiritual, does not command only external works but enjoins this especially—to love God with the whole heart.

No mention is made here of what is due to other people, and we should not regard this as unreasonable, for brotherly love flows immediately from the love of God, as we shall see in a moment. Whoever, then, wants their life to be approved by God must have all their doings directed to this end. If anyone objects and says that no one has ever been found who loved God perfectly, I reply that it is enough for everyone to aspire to this perfection according to the measure of grace given to them. In the meantime, the definition of the perfect love of God is the complete keeping of his law. To make progress in this as in knowledge is what we ought to do.

This is how we know we are in him. He is referring to that fruit of the Gospel that he had mentioned—fellowship with the Father and with the Son (1:3). Thus he confirms the previous sentence by stating what follows as a consequence. If it is the purpose of the Gospel to have communion with God, and no communion can exist without love, then no one makes real progress in faith unless he or she holds fast to God with the heart.

6. Whoever claims to live in him. As he has already given us the example of God as light, he now calls us also to Christ, that we may imitate him. Yet he does not simply exhort us to imitate Christ, but from the union we have with him he proves that we ought to be like him. A likeness in life and deeds, he says, will prove that we are in Christ. But from these words he passes on to the next clause, which he immediately adds, regarding love for our brothers.

7-11. Dear friends, I am not writing you a new command but an old one, which you have had since the beginning. This old command is the message you have heard. Yet I am writing you a new command; its truth is seen in him and you, because the darkness is passing and the true light is already shining. Anyone who claims to be in the light but

hates his brother is still in the darkness. Whoever loves his brother lives in the light, and there is nothing in him to make him stumble. But whoever hates his brother is in the darkness and walks around in the darkness; he does not know where he is going, because the darkness has blinded him.

7. Dear friends, I am not writing you a new command. This is an explanation of the preceding doctrine, that to love God is to keep his commandments. He had good reason to dwell on this point. First, we know that novelty is disliked or suspected. Second, we do not easily undertake any yoke we are not used to. In addition to these things, when we have embraced any kind of doctrine, we dislike having anything changed or made new in it. For these reasons John reminds us that he was teaching nothing but what had been heard by the faithful concerning love from the beginning and had become old through long usage.

Some people explain this oldness differently—that Christ now prescribes no other rule of life under the Gospel than what God did formerly under the law. This is indeed most true, but I think here John simply means that these were the first elements of the Gospel, which they had been taught from the beginning, and that there was no reason why they should reject as unusual what they ought to have been permeated with long since, for the relative seems to be used in a causative sense. So then, he calls it **old** not because it was taught to the fathers many ages before, but because it had been taught them on their very entrance into a religious life. And it served much to strengthen their faith that this had proceeded from Christ himself, from whom they had received the Gospel.

This old command. The word **old** here probably extends further, for the sentence is fuller: **which you have had since the beginning.** I think he means that the Gospel ought not to be received as a newborn doctrine but as something that has come from God and is his eternal truth. This is like saying, "You ought not to measure the antiquity of the Gospel that is brought to you by time, since the eternal will of God is revealed to you in it. Not only has God given you this rule of a holy life, when you were first called to the Christian faith, but this has always been prescribed and approved by him." Doubtless the only thing that should be deemed antiquity and deserves faith and reverence is what has its origin in God. For human fictions, however long they may have been around, cannot acquire so much authority that they subvert God's truth.

8. Yet I am writing you a new command. Many interpreters do not appear to me to have attained the apostle's meaning. He says **new** because God, as it were, renews it by daily suggesting it, so that the faithful may practice it through their whole life, for they can find nothing more excellent. The elements that children learn give place in time to what is higher and more solid. But John denies that the doctrine concerning brotherly love is of this kind, growing old with time; it is perpetually in force, so that it is the highest perfection just as much now as it was in the very beginning.

However, it was necessary to add this thought, for people are more curious than they should be, and there are many who always look for something new. They get tired of simple doctrine, and this produces innumerable errors when everyone gapes continually for new mysteries. When it is recognized that the Lord proceeds on the same even course, in order to keep us throughout life in what we have learned, a bridle is put on desires of this kind. So then, anyone who wants to reach the goal of wisdom about the right way of living should become proficient in love.

Its truth is seen in him and you ("which thing is true in him and in you," KJV). This proves what he had said, for this one command to love, concerning our conduct in life, constitutes the whole truth of Christ. Besides, what other greater revelation can be expected? No doubt Christ is the end and the completion of everything. Hence the word **truth** means that they stood, as it were, at the goal, for it is to be understood as a completion or a perfect state. The apostle sees Christ joined to them, just as the head is joined to the members. This is like saying that the body of the church has no other perfection, or that believers would be truly united to Christ if holy love existed among them continually.

Because the darkness is passing. He means that as soon as Christ brings light, we have the full brightness of knowledge: not that every one of the faithful becomes wise the first day as much as he ought to be (for even Paul testifies that he labored to apprehend what he had not apprehended— Philippians 3:12)), but that the knowledge of Christ alone is sufficient to dissipate darkness. Hence daily progress is necessary; and the faith of everyone has its dawn before it reaches the noonday. But as God continues to inculcate the same doctrine in which he bids us to advance, the knowledge of the Gospel is justly said to be the true light in which Christ, the Sun of Righteousness, shines. Thus the way is shut up against the audacity of those people who try to corrupt the purity of the Gospel by their own fictions.

9. Anyone who claims to be in the light. John continues to pursue the same metaphor. He said that love is the only true rule according to which our life is to be formed; he said that this rule or law is presented to us in the Gospel; he said, lastly, that it is like the noonday light and ought to be continually looked upon. Now, on the other hand, he concludes that everyone who is a stranger to love is blind and walks **in the darkness**. Before, he mentioned the love of God, and now he talks of loving the brothers, but this involves no contradiction, for these two are so connected that they cannot be separated.

In the third chapter John says that we falsely boast of love to God if we do not love our brothers, and this is most true. But now he takes love for the brothers as a testimony by which we prove that we love God. In short, since love so regards God that it embraces man, there is nothing strange when the apostle, speaking about love, refers at one time to God and at another to the brothers. This is what is commonly done in Scripture. The whole perfection of life is often said to consist in love for God. Paul teaches us that the whole law is fulfilled by him who loves his neighbor (Romans 13:8); and Christ declares that the most important matters of the law are "justice, mercy and faithfulness" (Matthew 23:23). Both these things are true and in agreement, for the love of God teaches us to love men; and we also in reality prove our love to God by loving men at his command. However this may be, it always remains certain that love is the rule of life. And this ought to be the more carefully noticed because people choose almost anything rather than this one commandment of God.

What follows comes to the same thing: **and there is nothing in him to make him stumble** (verse 10). That is, anyone who acts in love, anyone who lives like this, will never stumble.

11. But whoever hates his brother. Again John reminds us that whatever specious appearance of excellency you may show, there is still nothing but what is sinful if love is absent. This passage may be compared with 1 Corinthians 13, and no long explanation is needed. But this doctrine is not understood by the world because most people are dazzled by all sorts of masks or disguises. Thus, fictitious sanctity dazzles the eyes of almost everyone, while love is neglected or at least is driven to the farthest corner.

12-14. I write to you, dear children, because your sins have been for-

given on account of his name. I write to you, fathers, because you have known him who is from the beginning. I write to you, young men, because you have overcome the evil one. I write to you, dear children, because you have known the Father. I write to you, fathers, because you have known him who is from the beginning. I write to you, young men, because you are strong, and the word of God lives in you, and you have overcome the evil one.

12. Dear children. This is still a general declaration, for he is not addressing only those of tender age but people of all ages, as in verse 1, and also afterwards. I say this because interpreters have incorrectly applied the term to children. But John, when he speaks of children, called them *paidia*, a word that expresses age; but here, as a spiritual father, he calls the old as well as the young *teknia*. He will, indeed, presently address special words to different ages; yet it is a mistake to think that he begins to do so here. On the contrary, lest the previous exhortation should obscure the free pardon of sins, he again inculcates the doctrine that belongs uniquely to faith, in order that the foundation may always be retained with certainty—namely, that salvation is laid up for us in Christ alone.

Holiness of life ought indeed to be urged, the fear of God ought to be carefully enjoined, people ought to be sharply goaded to repentance, and newness of life, together with its fruits, ought to be recommended. But still we must always take heed lest the doctrine of faith be smothered—the necessary doctrine that teaches that Christ is the only author of salvation and of all blessings. On the contrary, such moderation ought to be presented that faith always retains its own primacy. This is the rule prescribed to us by John. Having faithfully spoken about good works, lest he should seem to give them more importance than he ought to have done, he carefully calls us back to contemplate the grace of Christ.

Your sins have been forgiven. Without this assurance, religion would only be fading and shadowy; indeed, those who ignore the free forgiveness of sins and dwell on other things build without a foundation. John tells us that nothing is better for stimulating fear of God than when people are rightly taught what a blessing Christ has brought to them, as Paul does when he urges people in view of God's mercies.

On account of his name. The actual cause is mentioned lest we should seek other means to reconcile us to God. For it would not be sufficient to know that God forgives us our sins unless we came directly to Christ and to the price that he paid on the cross for us. And this ought to be observed all the more because we see that by Satan's craft and by wicked human fictions, this way is obstructed; for foolish people attempt to pacify God by various satisfactions and devise innumerable kinds of expiations for the purpose of redeeming themselves. Every means of deserving pardon that we intrude on God is another obstacle that prevents us from approaching him. Hence John, not satisfied with simply stating the doctrine that God forgives our sins, expressly adds that God is propitious to us because he has regard for Christ, and so the apostle excludes all other reasons. We also, if we are to enjoy this blessing, must ignore and forget all other names and rely only on the name of Christ.

13. I write to you, fathers. He now comes to list different ages, so that he can show that what he taught suited every one of them. A general address produces less effect; we are so perverse that few of us think that what is addressed to everyone belongs to us. Old people mostly excuse themselves because they are past the age of learning; children refuse to learn, saying they are not yet old enough; the middle-aged do not pay attention because they are occupied with other things. So then, lest anyone should exempt themselves, the apostle mentions three ages, the most common divisions of human life.

He begins with the old and says that the Gospel is right for them because from it they learned to know the eternal Son of God. Moroseness is characteristic of the old, but they become especially unteachable because they measure wisdom by the number of years. Also, as Horace noted in his *Art of Poetry*, they praise the time of their youth and reject whatever is done or said differently. John wisely removes this evil when he reminds us that the Gospel contains not only a knowledge that is ancient but is also what leads us to the very eternity of God. Hence it follows that there is nothing here that they can dislike. John says that Christ was **from the beginning**; I take it this refers to his divine presence, as being coeternal with the Father, as well as to his power, of which the apostle speaks in Hebrew 13:8—he was yesterday what he is today. This is like saying, "If antiquity delights you, you have Christ, who is superior to all antiquity; his disciples ought not to be ashamed of him who includes all ages in himself."

We must also notice what sort of religion is really ancient—namely, that which is founded on Christ; for if religion derives its origin from error, it will be useless, however long it may have existed.

I write to you, young men. Though the Greek word is a diminutive, there is no doubt John is addressing all who were in the flower of their age. We also know that those of that age are so addicted to the vain cares of the world that they think little of the kingdom of God, for the vigor of their minds and the strength of their bodies make them drunk, as it were. The apostle, then, reminds them where true strength comes from, so that they might no longer exult as usual in the flesh. **You are strong,** he says (verse 14), **because you have overcome the evil one**—that is, Satan (verse 13). Doubtless the strength we ought to seek is spiritual. And the apostle says that it is not to be had except from Christ, for he mentions the blessings that we receive through the Gospel. He says that people who have conquered are still engaged in the battle; but our condition is quite different from that of those who are fighting under human banners, for the outcome of war is uncertain to them, whereas we are conquerors before we engage with the enemy, for our head, Christ, has once for all conquered the whole world for us.

I write to you, dear children. They had to be addressed explicitly. The apostle concludes that the Gospel is well adapted to young children because they find **the Father** in it. We now see how diabolical it is to drive all ages away from the doctrine of the Gospel, though the Spirit of God so carefully addresses them all.

But these things that the apostle makes particular are also general, for we should wholly fall off into vanity if our weakness were not strengthened by God's eternal truth. There is nothing in us that is not frail and fading, unless Christ's power dwells in us. We are all like orphans until we reach the grace of adoption by the Gospel. Hence, what he declares respecting young children is also true for the old. But still his object was to apply to each group what was most especially necessary for them, that he might show that they all without exception needed the doctrine of the Gospel.

15-17. Do not love the world or anything in the world. If anyone loves the world, the love of the Father is not in him. For everything in the world—the cravings of sinful man, the lust of his eyes and the boasting of what he has and does—comes not from the Father but from the world. The world and its desires pass away, but the man who does the will of God lives forever.

15. Do not love. John has already said that the only rule for living religiously is to love God; but when we are occupied with the vain love of the world, we turn all our thoughts and affections another way. This vanity must be torn away from us first, in order that the love of God may reign within us. Until our minds are cleansed, the former doctrine may be repeated a hundred times, but without effect; it would be like pouring water on a ball—you cannot collect one drop, because there is no empty place to hold the water.

The world means everything connected with the present life, apart from the kingdom of God and the hope of eternal life. So he includes in it corruptions of every kind and the abyss of all evils. In the world are pleasures, delights, and all those attractions by which people are so captivated that they withdraw from God.

Moreover, love of the world is severely condemned in this way because we necessarily forget God and ourselves when we regard nothing so much as this earth; when a corrupt lust of this kind rules in us and so holds us entangled that we do not think about the heavenly life, we are possessed by an animal stupidity.

If anyone loves the world. By arguing from what is contrary, John proves how necessary it is to get rid of love of the world if we want to please God; and this he later confirms by an argument drawn from what is inconsistent, for what belongs to the world is wholly at variance with God. We must bear in mind what I have already said, that a corrupt mode of life is mentioned here that has nothing in common with the kingdom of God— that is, a life in which people become so degenerate that they are satisfied with the present life and think no more of immortal life than mute animals. So then, whoever makes himself a slave to earthly lusts in this way cannot be of God.

16. The cravings of sinful man, the lust of his eyes and the boasting of what he has and does. John, by way of explanation, inserted these three particulars as examples, that he might briefly show what are the pursuits and thoughts of people who live for the world; but whether it is a full and complete division does not matter much, though you will not find a worldly person in whom at least one of these lusts does not prevail. It remains for us to see what he understands by each of these.

The first clause, **the cravings of sinful man,** is commonly explained as all sinful lusts in general, for the reference is to the whole corrupt nature of humankind. I am reluctant to argue the point, but I also do not want to disguise the fact that I favor another meaning. Paul, when in Romans 13:14 he forbids us to make provision for "the desires of the sinful nature," seems to me to be the best interpreter of this passage. What is "the sinful nature" there? It is the body and all that belongs to it. What, then, are the desires of the sinful nature but when worldly people seek to live softly and delicately and are intent only on their own advantages? Epicurus made a threefold division between desires: he made some natural and necessary, some natural and not necessary, and some neither natural nor necessary. But John, who well knew the insubordination of the human heart, unhesitatingly condemns the desires of the sinful nature because they are always excessive and never observe any due moderation. He afterwards comes gradually to grosser vices.

The lust of his eyes. I think John includes libidinous looks as well as the vanity that delights in pomp and empty splendor.

Lastly follows **boasting** or haughtiness, with which is connected ambition, contempt of others, blind love of self, and headstrong self-confidence.

The sum total is that as soon as the world presents itself, our lusts and desires, when our heart is corrupt, are captivated by it, like unbridled wild beasts, so that various lusts, all of them against God, rule in us.

17. The world and its desires pass away. As everything in the world is fading and ephemeral, John concludes that those who seek happiness from it make a wretched and miserable provision for themselves, especially when God calls us to the ineffable glory of eternal life. This is like saying, "The true happiness that God offers to his children is eternal; it is then a shameful thing for us to be entangled with the world, which with all its benefits will soon vanish away." I take **desires** here to mean what is desired or coveted, or what captivates our desires. The meaning is that what is most precious in the world and is deemed especially desirable is nothing but a shadowy phantom.

By saying that those who obey God will live **forever** or perpetually, he means that those who seek God will be perpetually blessed. If anyone objects that no one does what God commands, the obvious answer is that what is spoken of here is not the perfect keeping of the law but the obedience of faith, which, however imperfect it may be, is still approved by God. The will of God is first made known to us in the law; but as no one satisfies the law, no happiness can be hoped for from it. But Christ comes to meet the despairing with new aid, not only regenerating us by his Spirit so that we may obey God, but also making this endeavor of ours, such as it is, obtain the praise of perfect righteousness.

18-19. Dear children, this is the last hour; and as you have heard that the antichrist is coming, even now many antichrists have come. This is how we know it is the last hour. They went out from us, but they did not really belong to us. For if they had belonged to us, they would have remained with us; but their going showed that none of them belonged to us.

18. This is the last hour. John fortifies the faithful against offenses by which they might have been disturbed. Already many sects had risen up that broke the unity of faith and caused disorder in the churches. But the apostle not only strengthens the faithful, lest they should falter, but turns the situation to an opposite effect, for he reminds them that **the last hour** had already come, and therefore he exhorts them to a greater vigilance. This is like saying, "While various errors are arising, it is right for you to be awakened rather than to be overwhelmed; for we ought to conclude from this that Christ is not far off. Let us then attentively look for him, lest he should come upon us suddenly." In the same way it is right for us to comfort ourselves today and to see by faith the nearness of Christ, while Satan is causing confusion for the sake of disturbing the church, for these are the signs of **the last hour.**

So many ages having passed since the death of John seems to prove that this prophecy is not true. To this I answer that the apostle, according to the usual method adopted in the Scripture, declares to the faithful that nothing more now remained but that Christ should appear for the redemption of the world. But as he fixes no time, he did not woo the people of that age by a vain hope, nor did he intend to cut short the future course of the church and the many successions of years during which the church has hitherto remained in the world. And no doubt, if the eternity of God's kingdom is borne in mind, such a long time will appear to us as a moment. We must understand the apostle's aim; namely, he means by **the last hour** the time in which everything will be so completed that nothing will remain except the final revelation of Christ.

As you have heard that the antichrist is coming. He speaks as though this is something well known; so we may conclude that the faithful had been taught and warned from the beginning about the future disorder of the church, in order that they might carefully keep themselves in the faith they professed, and also instruct posterity in the duty of watchfulness. For it was God's will that his church should be tried like this, lest anyone knowingly and willingly should be deceived, and so there might be no excuse for ignorance. But we see that almost the whole world has been miserably deceived, as though not a word had been said about Antichrist.

Even now many antichrists have come. This may seem to have been added by way of correction, but it is not so. Those who supposed that Antichrist would be only one man are indeed greatly mistaken, for Paul, referring to a future defection, plainly shows that it would involve a certain body or kingdom (2 Thessalonians 2:3). Paul first predicts a defection that would prevail through the whole church, a universal evil; he then makes the head of the apostasy the adversary of Christ, who would sit in the temple of God claiming for himself divinity and divine honors. Unless we deliberately choose another wrong way, we may learn from Paul's description how to recognize Antichrist.

But how can that passage agree with John's saying that there were already **many antichrists?** To this I answer that John simply meant that some particular sects had already arisen that were forerunners of a future Antichrist. Strictly speaking, Antichrist was not yet in existence; but the mystery of iniquity was working secretly. John uses the name so that he might effectively stimulate the care and solicitude of the godly in order to repel frauds.

But if God's Spirit even then commanded the faithful to stand watch, when they only saw distant signs of the coming enemy, how much less is it now time for us to sleep.

19. They went out from us. John anticipates another objection, that the church seemed to have produced these pests and to have cherished them for a time. Certainly it serves more to disturb the weak when anyone among us, professing the true faith, falls away than when a thousand outsiders conspire against us. He then confesses that they had gone *out from* the heart of the church, but he denies that they were ever *of* the church. The way to remove this objection is to say that the church is always exposed to this evil, so that it is constrained to bear with many hypocrites who do not really know Christ, however much they may profess his name with their words.

By saying **They went out from us,** he means that they had previously occupied a place in the church and were counted among the number of the godly. However, he denies that they were of them, though they had assumed the name of believers, just as chaff is mixed with wheat on the same floor but cannot be regarded as wheat.

For if they had belonged to us. John plainly declares that those who fell away had never been members of the church. And doubtless the seal of God, under which he keeps his own, remains sure, as Paul says (2 Timothy 2:19). But there is a difficulty here, for it happens that many people who seemed to have embraced Christ often fall away. To this I answer that there are three sorts of people who profess the Gospel. There are those who feign piety, while a bad conscience reproves them within; others, whose hypocrisy is more deceptive, not only try to disguise themselves before other people but also dazzle their own eyes, so that they seem to themselves to worship God correctly; the third sort are those who have the living root of faith and carry a testimony of their own adoption firmly fixed in their hearts. The first two have no stability. It is the last group that Scripture speaks about when it says it is impossible for them to be separated from the church, for the seal that God's Spirit engraves on their hearts cannot be obliterated; the incorruptible seed that has taken root cannot be pulled up or destroyed.

John is not speaking here about the constancy of human beings but about God, whose election will certainly be confirmed. So it is not without reason that he declares that where the calling of God is effectual, perseverance is certain. In short, he means that those who fall away have never been thoroughly imbued with the knowledge of Christ but only had a brief and transient taste of it.

Their going showed that none of them belonged to us. He shows that examining one's faith to be sure it is genuine is useful and necessary for the church. Hence it follows, on the other hand, that there is no good reason for being perturbed. Since the church is like a threshing floor, the chaff must be blown away in order for the pure wheat to remain. This is what God does when he throws hypocrites out of the church, for then he is cleansing it of refuse and filth.

20-23. But you have an anointing from the Holy One, and all of you know the truth. I do not write to you because you do not know the truth, but because you do know it and because no lie comes from the truth. Who is the liar? It is the man who denies that Jesus is the Christ. Such a man is the antichrist—he denies the Father and the Son. No one who denies the Son has the Father; whoever acknowledges the Son has the Father also.

20. But you have an anointing. The apostle modestly excuses himself for warning them so earnestly, lest they should think they were being indirectly reproved, as though they were ignorant of those things that they ought to have known well. So also Paul conceded wisdom to the Romans, saying that they were able and fit to admonish others. At the same time he showed that they needed to be reminded in order that they might do their duty properly (Romans 15:14-15). The apostles did not, however, speak like this in order to flatter people; they were wisely being careful that their teaching was not needlessly rejected by anyone, for they were telling them things that were appropriate and useful not only to ignorant people but also to those well instructed in the Lord's school.

Experience teaches us how overly demanding people are. Such capricious standards ought indeed to be far from godly people, and yet it is advisable for a faithful and wise teacher not to omit anything that will get a hearing from others. We must certainly give less attention and respect to what is said when the knowledge the Lord has given us is being disparaged.

So the apostle did not teach his readers as though they were ignorant, acquainted only with the rudiments of knowledge, but was reminding them of what they already knew and was also exhorting them to rouse up the sparks of the Spirit so that a full brightness might shine in them. And in the next words he explains himself: he denies that he wrote to them because they did not know the truth, but because they had been well taught in it, for if they had been wholly ignorant and novices, they could not have understood his teaching.

An anointing from the Holy One. The oil by which the priests were anointed was obtained from the sanctuary, and Daniel mentions the coming of Christ as the proper time for anointing the Most Holy (Daniel 9:24). For Christ was anointed by the Father in order that he might pour out on us a great abundance from his own fullness. Hence it follows that people are not really made wise by the acumen of their own minds but by the illumination of the Spirit; furthermore, we do not share in the Spirit except through Christ, who is the true sanctuary and our only High Priest.

21. And because no lie comes from the truth. John gives them a rule by which they could distinguish truth from falsehood. It is not the dialectic proposition that falsehood differs from truth; rather, what he says is applied to what is practical and useful. This is like saying that they not only held what was true but were also so strengthened against the fallacies of ungodly people that they wisely took care of themselves. The apostle does not speak about any particular kind of falsehood but says that whatever deception Satan might contrive, or in whatever way he might attack them, they would be able to distinguish readily between light and darkness because they had the Spirit as their guide.

22. Who is the liar? John does not assert that only those who denied that the Son of God had appeared in the flesh were liars, but that those deceivers surpassed all others. This is like saying that if *this* is not considered a lie, nothing else could be called a lie either, just as we often say, "If infidelity toward God and man is not a crime, what else can we call a crime?"

What he had said in a general way about false prophets he now applies to the state of his own time. He points out, as if with his finger, those who disturbed the church. I readily agree with the ancient writers who thought that the reference here is to Cerinthus and Carpocrates. But the denial of Christ extends much wider. It is not enough to confess in words that Jesus is the Christ, unless he is acknowledged to be such as the Father offers him to us in the Gospel. The two I have named gave the title of Christ to the Son of God but imagined him to be only human. Others followed them, such as Arius, who, while giving him the name of God, robbed him of his eternal deity. Marcion dreamed that Christ was a mere phantom. Sabellius imagined that he did not differ from the Father in any way. All these denied the Son of God, for not one of them really acknowledged the true Christ. As far as they could, they adulterated the truth about him, devising an idol for themselves instead of Christ. Then Pelagius came along, raising no question about Christ's essence, but accepting him as true man and God; yet he transferred to us almost all the honor that belongs to him. Indeed, when Christ's grace and power are set aside, Christ is reduced to nothing.

So also today, some people set up free will in opposition to the grace of the Holy Spirit, ascribing part of their righteousness and salvation to the merits of works, imagining they have innumerable advocates by whom they can make God propitious to them, and having a fictitious sort of Christ. But the living and genuine image of God, which shines in Christ, they deform by their wicked ideas; they lessen his power and subvert and pervert his office.

We now see that Christ is denied whenever people take away from him what is uniquely his. And as Christ is the goal of the law and of the Gospel and has in himself all the treasures of wisdom and knowledge, he is the target at which all heretics level and direct their arrows. Therefore, the apostle has good reason to regard as the chief impostors those who fight against Christ, in whom the full truth is revealed to us.

Such a man is the antichrist. John is not speaking about the prince of defection who will occupy God's seat, but about all those who seek to overthrow Christ. In order to magnify their crime, he asserts that the Father, no less than the Son, is denied by them (verses 22-23). This is like saying that they no longer have any religion because they throw God away completely. And he later confirms this by adding this reason, that the Father cannot be separated from the Son (verse 23).

Now this is a remarkable sentence and ought to be reckoned among the first axioms of our religion. Indeed, when we have confessed that there is one true God, this second article of faith ought necessarily to be added, that he is none other but he who is made known in Christ. The apostle here does not deal distinctly with the unity of essence. Indeed, it is certain that the Son cannot be separated from the Father, for he is of the same essence. But something else is spoken of here—namely, that the Father, who is invisible, has revealed himself only in his Son. Hence Christ is called the image of the Father (Hebrews 1:3) because he sets forth and exhibits to us all that is necessary for us to know about the Father. God's sheer majesty would, by its immense brightness, always dazzle our eyes; it is therefore necessary for us to look at Christ. This is to come to the light that otherwise is rightly said to be inaccessible.

Again I say that there is no distinct discussion here of the eternal essence of Christ that he has in common with the Father. This passage is, indeed, quite sufficient to prove it; but John is calling us to a practical part of faith—namely, that as God has given himself to us to be enjoyed only in Christ, we seek him in vain elsewhere. Or if you prefer, all the fullness of the Deity is to be found in Christ, and there is no God apart from him. Hence it follows that Muslims, Jews, and such like have a mere idol and not the true God. For by whatever name they may honor the God whom they worship, still, as they reject Christ, without whom they cannot come to God, and in whom God has truly revealed himself, what do they have but some creation or fiction of their own? People may flatter themselves with their own speculations as much as they please, philosophizing on divine things without Christ; but it is still certain that they are only ranting and raving because, as Paul says, they have "lost connection with the Head" (Colossians 2:19). Hence it is obvious how necessary it is to know Christ.

23. Whoever acknowledges the Son has the Father also. There is no right confession of God without the Father being acknowledged in the Son.

If anyone objects that many people in ancient times thought rightly of God, though they did not know Christ, I admit that the knowledge of Christ has not always been revealed so explicitly. Nevertheless, I contend that it has always been true that just as the light of the sun comes to us by its rays, so the knowledge of God has been communicated through Christ.

24-29. See that what you have heard from the beginning remains in you. If it does, you also will remain in the Son and in the Father. And this is what he promised to us—even eternal life. I am writing these things to you about those who are trying to lead you astray. As for you, the anointing you received from him remains in you, and you do not need anyone to teach you. But as his anointing teaches you about all things and as that anointing is real, not counterfeit—just as it has taught you, remain in him. And now, dear children, continue in him, so that when he appears we may be confident and unashamed before him at his coming. If you know that he is righteous, you know that every- one who does what is right has been born of him.

24. See that what you have heard . . . remains in you. To the above doctrine John adds an exhortation, and, so it has more weight, he points out the fruit they would receive from obedience. He then urges them to persevere in the faith, so that what they had learned might remain fixed in their hearts.

From the beginning. He does not mean that antiquity alone was enough to prove the truth of any doctrine. He has already shown that they have been rightly taught the pure Gospel of Christ, and now he concludes that they ought rightly to continue in it. And this order ought to be espe- cially noticed, for if we are unwilling to depart from doctrine once we have embraced it, whatever it is, without confirming it by the Word of God, that would not be perseverance but perverse obstinacy. Hence we should exer- cise discrimination, so that a reason for our faith may be made evident from God's Word; *then* let inflexible perseverance follow. If we imbibe supersti- tions from childhood and then boast about **the beginning,** we will thus allow ourselves obstinately to reject clear truth. Such perverseness shows that we must always begin with the certainty of truth.

If it does. Here is the fruit of perseverance: those in whom God's truth remains, remain in God. From this we learn what we are to seek in any truth pertaining to religion. The person who is the most proficient is the one who makes such progress as to cling wholly to God. But anyone in whom the Father does not dwell thorough his Son is altogether vain and empty, whatever knowledge he may possess. Moreover, the highest commendation of sound doctrine is that it unites us to God and that in it is found whatever pertains to the real experience of God.

Lastly, he reminds us that it is real happiness when God lives in us. We cannot live except by nourishing to the end the seed of life sown in our hearts. John insists much on the point that not only the beginning of a blessed life is to be found in the knowledge of Christ, but also its perfection. But no repetition of this can be too much, since it is well known that it has always been a cause of ruin when people are not content with Christ and wander beyond the simple doctrine of the Gospel.

26. I am writing these things to you. The apostle excuses himself again for having admonished people who had plenty of knowledge and judgment. But he did this so that they might ask for the Spirit's guidance, in case his warning was in vain. This was like saying, "I indeed do my part, but still it is necessary for the Spirit of God to direct you in everything; for it is no good to have my voice sounding in your ears, or rather in the air, unless he speaks within you."

When we hear that he wrote about seducers, we should always bear in mind that it is the duty of a good and diligent pastor not only to gather a flock but also to drive wolves away; for what good will it be for us to proclaim the pure Gospel if we fail to oppose Satan's counterfeits? No one, then, can faithfully teach the church if he is not diligent in banishing errors whenever he finds them spread by seducers. I take what John says about **his anointing** (verse 27) to refer to Christ.

27. And you do not need anyone to teach you. As I have already said, John's purpose would indeed be strange if he had intended to represent teaching as useless. He did not ascribe to them so much wisdom as to deny that they were Christ's pupils. He only meant that they were by no means so ignorant as to need unknown things, as it were, taught to them, and that he did not set before them anything that the Spirit of God might not himself suggest to them. It is absurd, then, for fanatics to seize on this passage to exclude outward ministry from the church. The apostle says that the faithful, taught by the Spirit, already understood what he was bringing to them, so that they had no need to learn things unknown to them. He said this so that he might add more authority to his doctrine, as everyone assented to it in his heart—engraved there, as it were, by God's finger. But as everyone had knowledge in proportion to their faith, and as faith in some of them was small and in others stronger, and in none of them was it perfect, so it follows that no one knew so much that there was no room for progress.

There is also another use to be made of this doctrine—that when people really understand what is needed, we still have to warn and rouse them, so that they may be strengthened all the more. John says that they were taught everything by the Spirit, but this should not be taken generally but should be confined to what is contained in this passage. In short, he had no other aim but to strengthen their faith as he recalled them to the examination of the Spirit, who is the only fit corrector and approver of doctrine and who seals it on our hearts, so that we may certainly know that God is speaking. For while faith ought to look to God, he alone can be a witness to himself, so as to convince our hearts that what our ears receive has come from him.

That is the meaning of the words, **as his anointing teaches you about all things and as that anointing is real.** That is, the Spirit is like a seal by which the truth of God is testified to us. When he adds **not counterfeit,** he is pointing out another function of the Spirit, and that is that he gives us judgment and discernment, so that we are not deceived by lies or should hesitate and be perplexed or vacillate in doubtful things.

Just as it has taught you, remain in him. He has said that the Spirit remained in them; he now exhorts them to remain in the revelation made by him, and he specifies what revelation it was. "Remain in Christ," he says, "as the Spirit has taught you." Another explanation, I know, is often given: "Abide in it"—that is, in the anointing. But as the repetition that immediately follows cannot apply to anything except Christ, I have no doubt that here too John is speaking about Christ. This is required by the context, for the apostle dwells much on the point that the faithful should retain the true knowledge of Christ and should not go to God in any other way.

At the same time, he shows that God's children are illuminated by the Spirit simply in order that they may know Christ. Provided they did not turn aside from him, Christ promised them the fruit of perseverance—that is, confidence—so that they will not be ashamed in his presence. Faith is not a mere cold apprehension of Christ, but a living and real sense of his power, which produces confidence. Indeed, faith cannot stand unless it looks to the coming of Christ and, supported by his power, brings tranquillity to the conscience. But the nature of confidence is well expressed when John says that it can boldly sustain the presence of Christ. Those who indulge in their vices without a care are in effect turning their backs on God; nor can they obtain peace in any other way but by forgetting him. This is the security of the flesh, which stupefies people, so that, turning away from God, they neither dread nor fear death; and in the meantime they shun Christ's tribunal. But a godly conscience delights to look at God. Thus godly people calmly wait for Christ and do not dread his coming.

29. If you know that he is righteous. Again John passes on to exhortations; he mingles these continually with doctrine throughout the letter. But he proves by many arguments that faith is necessarily connected with a holy and pure life. The first argument is that we are spiritually born in the likeness of Christ; hence it follows that no one is born of Christ but those who live righteously. At the same time, it is uncertain whether he means Christ or God when he says that those who are **born of him** do **what is right**. It is certainly a manner of speaking used in Scripture that we are born of God in Christ; but there is nothing wrong with the other interpretation, that those who are renewed by his Spirit are born of Christ.

Chapter 3

1-3. How great is the love the Father has lavished on us, that we should be called children of God! And that is what we are! The reason the world does not know us is that it did not know him. Dear friends, now we are children of God, and what we will be has not yet been made known. But we know that when he appears, we shall be like him, for we shall see him as he is. Everyone who has this hope in him purifies himself, just as he is pure.

1. The second argument is from the dignity and excellence of our calling, for it was no common honor, John says, that the heavenly Father bestowed on us when he adopted us as his children. As this is such a great favor, it should kindle in us a desire for purity, so that we are conformed to his image. And it must be that anyone who acknowledges himself to be one of God's children should purify himself. To reinforce this exhortation, the apostle emphasizes God's favor; for when he says that **love** has been **lavished on us**, he means that it is from mere bounty and benevolence that God makes us his children. Where do we obtain such dignity unless it is from God's love?

Love, then, is declared here to be free. In short, he means that the more abundantly God's goodness has been revealed to us, the greater are our obligations to him; compare Paul's teaching when he urged the Romans in view of God's mercy to offer themselves as living sacrifices to him (Romans 12:1). At the same time, we are taught that the adoption of all godly people is free and does not depend in any way on works.

The Sophists say that God foresees those who are worthy of adoption, but this is plainly refuted by these words, for in that case the gift would not be free. We must understand this doctrine especially, for since the only cause of our salvation is adoption, and since the apostle testifies that this flows simply from the love of God, there is nothing left of our worthiness or the merits of works. Why are we God's children? Because God began to love us freely when we deserved hatred rather than love. And as the Spirit is a pledge of our adoption, it follows that any good in us ought not to be set up in opposition to God's grace, but on the contrary to be ascribed to him.

When he says that we are **called** or named, he means that it is God himself who declares us to be his children, just as he gave a name to Abraham according to what he was.

The reason the world does not know us. It is a trial that grievously assaults our faith that we are not so much regarded as God's children or that no mark of such great excellence appears in us but that, on the contrary, almost the whole world treats us with ridicule and contempt. Hence it can hardly be inferred from our present state that God is a Father to us, for the devil so contrives everything that it obscures this benefit. John answers this offense by saying that we are not as yet acknowledged to be what we are, because the world does not know God. Remarkable examples of this very thing are found in Isaac and Jacob; for though both were chosen by God, Ishmael persecuted Isaac with laughter and taunts, and Esau persecuted Jacob with threats and the sword. So, however we may be oppressed by the world, our salvation still remains safe and secure.

2. Now we are children of God. John now comes to what everyone knows and feels himself, for though the ungodly may not entice us to give up our hope, yet our present condition is far short of the glory of God's children; for as far as our body is concerned we are dust and a shadow, and death is always before our eyes. We are also subject to a thousand miseries, and the soul is exposed to innumerable evils, so that we always find a hell within us. It is all the more necessary that our thoughts should be withdrawn from the present view of things, so that the miseries that surround and almost overwhelm us on every side will not shake our faith in the happiness that is as yet hidden. The apostle means that we act very foolishly when we estimate what God has bestowed upon us according to the present state of things, and that we ought with undoubting faith to hold on to what does not yet appear.

But we know that when he appears. John teaches the same thing as Paul does in Colossians 3:3-4, where he says, "Your life is now hidden with Christ in God. When Christ, who is your life, appears, then you also will appear with him in glory." Our faith cannot stand in any other way but by looking to the coming of Christ. The reason God defers the manifestation of our glory is because Christ has not yet been revealed in the power of his kingdom. So then, this is the only way of sustaining our faith, so that we may wait patiently for the life promised to us. As soon as anyone turns away in the least from Christ, he must necessarily fail.

The word **know** shows the certainty of faith, in order to distinguish it from opinion. Neither simple nor universal knowledge is meant here, but that which everyone ought to have for himself, so that he may feel assured that he will someday be like Christ. So then, though the manifestation of our glory is connected with the coming of Christ, our knowledge of this is well-founded.

We shall be like him. John does not mean that we shall be equal to him, for there must be some difference between the Head and the members; but **we shall be like him** because he will make our vile body "like his glorious body," as Paul teaches us in Philippians 3:21. John intended to show that the final end of our adoption is that what has happened first of all with Christ will in the end be completed in us.

The reason that is added may, however, seem inappropriate, for if to **see** Christ makes us **like** him, we shall have this in common with the wicked, for they too will see his glory. To this I reply that this is to see him as a friend, which will not be the case with the wicked, for they will dread his presence. Indeed, they will shun God's presence and be filled with terror; his glory will so dazzle their eyes that they will be stupefied and confounded. We see that Adam, conscious of having done wrong, dreaded the presence of God. And God declared through Moses, as a general truth about mankind, "No one may see me and live" (Exodus 33:20). How can it be otherwise than that God's majesty, as a consuming fire, will consume us as though we were stubble, so great is the weakness of our flesh. But as the image of God is renewed in us, our eyes are prepared to see God. And now, indeed, God is beginning to renew his image in us—but in what a small measure! So unless we are stripped of all the corruption of the flesh, we shall not be able to see God face to face.

This is also expressed in the words **just as he is pure** (verse 3). John is not saying there is no seeing of God now; but as Paul says, "Now we see but a poor reflection," as in a mirror (1 Corinthians 13:12). Elsewhere, he makes a distinction between this way of living and the seeing of the eye. In short, God now presents himself to be seen by us, not as he is, but in a way we can understand. Thus Moses' saying is fulfilled—we see his back, as it were (Exodus 33:23), for there is too much brightness in his face.

We must also notice that the way the apostle mentions is taken from the effect, not from the cause; for he does not teach us that we shall **be like him** because we shall **see him**, but he proves that we shall share the divine glory, for unless our nature were spiritual and endued with a heavenly and blessed immortality, it could never come so near to God. Yet the perfection of glory will not be so great in us that our seeing will enable us to comprehend all that God is, for the distance between us and him will even then be very great.

But when the apostle says that **we shall see him as he is,** he intimates a new and indescribable manner of seeing him, which we do not enjoy now. As long as we walk by faith, as Paul teaches, we are absent from him. And when God appeared to the fathers, it was not in his own essence, but he was always seen symbolically. Hence the majesty of God, now hidden, will only be seen in itself when the veil of this mortal and corruptible nature is removed.

I shall pass over questions about details, for we see how Augustine tormented himself with these and yet never succeeded, both in his letters to Paulus and Fortunatus and in his *City of God* (ii.2) and in other places. What he says, however, is worth noticing: the way in which we live helps such an inquiry more than the way in which we speak, and we must beware lest by arguing about the way in which God can be seen, we lose that peace and holiness without which no one will see him.

3. Everyone who has this hope. John now draws the inference that the desire for holiness should not grow cold in us because our happiness has not yet appeared, for that hope is enough. And indeed we know that what is hoped for is hidden as yet. The meaning is that though we do not have Christ present before our eyes now, if we hope in him, our hope must excite and stimulate us to follow purity, for it leads us straight to Christ, whom we know to be a perfect pattern of purity.

4-6. Everyone who sins breaks the law; in fact, sin is lawlessness. But you know that he appeared so that he might take away our sins. And in

him is no sin. No one who lives in him keeps on sinning. No one who continues to sin has either seen him or known him.

4. Everyone who sins. The apostle has already shown how ungrateful we must be to God if we make little of the honor of adoption, by which he of his own goodwill chooses us, and if we do not offer him our love in return. He also introduced the warning that our love ought not to be diminished because the promised happiness is deferred. But now, as people indulge themselves in evil more than they should, he reproves a perverse indulgence, declaring that all who sin are wicked and are transgressors of the law. Probably there were those at that time who extenuated their vices by this kind of flattery: "It is no wonder that we sin, because we are human; but there is a great difference between sin and iniquity."

The apostle now deals with this frivolous excuse by defining sin as a transgression of the divine law. His object was to produce hatred and horror of sin. The word **sin** seems light to some people, but iniquity or transgression of the law cannot be so easily forgiven. The apostle does not make sins equal by saying that everyone who sins commits iniquity. He simply wants to teach us that sin arises from a contempt of God and that by sinning, the law is violated. Hence this doctrine of John has nothing in common with the mad paradoxes of the Stoics.

Besides, the word **sins** here does not mean to offend only in some instances; nor is the word to be taken for every fault or wrong a person may commit. He calls it **sin** when people with their whole heart run into evil. For the faithful, who are as yet tempted by the lusts of the flesh, are not to be deemed guilty of iniquity, though they are not pure or free from sin; but as sin does not *reign* in them, John says that they do not sin, as I shall presently explain more fully.

The import of the passage is that the perverse life of those who indulge themselves in the liberty of sinning is hateful to God and cannot be borne with by him, because it is contrary to his law. It does not follow, nor can it be inferred, from this that the faithful are iniquitous, because they desire to obey God and abhor their own vices; they also form their own life, as far as they can, according to the law. But when there is a deliberate intention to sin, or a continued course in sin, then the law is transgressed.

5. But you know that he appeared. John shows by another argument how much sin and faith differ from one another, for it is Christ's function to take away sins, and for this purpose he was sent by the Father; and it is by faith that we share in Christ's virtue. So then, anyone who believes in Christ is necessarily cleansed from sins. But it says in John 1:29 that Christ takes away sins because he atones for them by the sacrifice of his death, so that they may not be imputed to us before God. John means in this passage that Christ actually takes away sins because through him our old self is crucified, and his Spirit, by means of repentance, mortifies the flesh with all its lusts. The context does not allow us to refer this to the remission of sins. Rather, he reasons thus: "Those who do not cease to sin render void the benefits derived from Christ, since he came to destroy the reigning power of sin." This belongs to the sanctification of the Spirit.

And in him is no sin. He is not speaking about Christ personally but of his whole body. John denies that there is any more room for sin wherever Christ diffuses his efficacious grace. Therefore, he immediately draws the inference that those who remain in Christ do not sin, for if he lives in us by faith, he cleanses us from sins. Christ by his Spirit does not perfectly renew us at once or in an instant, but he continues our renovation throughout life on earth. The faithful are exposed to sin as long as they live in the world, but as far as the kingdom of Christ prevails in them, sin is abolished. In the meantime they are designated according to the prevailing principle; that is, they are said to be righteous and to live righteously because they sincerely aspire to righteousness.

6. No one who lives in him. John says that the faithful live in Christ because we are united to him by faith and are made one with him.

Keeps on sinning. They are said not to sin because they do not consent to sin, though they do labor under the infirmity of the flesh; in fact, they struggle with groaning, so that they can truly testify with Paul that they do the evil they do not want to do.

No one who continues to sin has either seen him or known him. According to his usual manner John adds the opposite clause, so that we may know that it is in vain to claim faith in Christ and knowledge of him unless there is newness of life. Christ is never dormant where he reigns, but the Spirit makes his power effective. It may rightly be said of him that he puts sin to flight, just as the sun drives darkness away by its own brightness. Again this passage teaches us how strong and efficacious the knowledge of Christ is, for it transforms us into his image. So by seeing and knowing in this verse we are to understand nothing other than faith.

7-10a. Dear children, do not let anyone lead you astray. He who does

what is right is righteous, just as he is righteous. He who does what is sinful is of the devil, because the devil has been sinning from the beginning. The reason the Son of God appeared was to destroy the devil's work. No one who is born of God will continue to sin, because God's seed remains in him; he cannot go on sinning, because he has been born of God. This is how we know who the children of God are and who the children of the devil are.

7. He who does what is right. Here the apostle shows that newness of life is manifested by good works. The likeness of which he has spoken (that is, between Christ and his followers) appears only by the fruits they produce. This is like saying, "Since it behooves us to be conformed to Christ, the truth and evidence of this must appear in our life." The exhortation is the same as Paul's in Galatians 5:25: "Since we live by the Spirit, let us keep in step with the Spirit." Many people would gladly persuade themselves that they have this righteousness buried in their hearts, even though iniquity occupies their feet and hands and tongue and eyes.

8. He who does what is sinful. This word **does** also refers to outward works, meaning that there is no life of God and of Christ where people act perversely and wickedly; on the contrary, such people are the devil's slaves. By this way of speaking John shows more fully how unlike Christ they are. For as he has already represented Christ as the fountain of all righteousness, so now he mentions the devil as the beginning of sin. He denies that anyone belongs to Christ except for those who are righteous and show themselves to be such by their works; and he assigns all others to the devil and subjects them to his government, in order that we may know there is no middle condition, but that Satan exercises his tyranny where the righteousness of Christ does not have the primacy.

However, there are not two opposing principles in the universe, as the Manicheans imagined. We know that the devil is not wicked by original nature or by creation but became so by defecting. We also know that he is not equal to God, so that he can contend with him with equal right or authority; rather, he is under restraint, so that he can do nothing unless his Creator permits it. John says that some are born of God and some of the devil; he means that the former are governed and guided by the Spirit of God, and the others are led astray by Satan, as God allows him this power over unbelievers.

Because the devil has been sinning from the beginning. As earlier

John did not speak about Christ personally when he said that he is right-eous, but mentioned him as the fountain and the cause of righteousness, so now when he says that the devil sins, he includes his whole body—that is, all the reprobate. This is like saying that it is the devil's work to entice people to sin. Hence it follows that his members, and all who are ruled by him, give themselves to committing sin. But the **beginning** that the apostle mentions is not from eternity, as when he says the Word is from the beginning, for there is a great difference between God and creatures. **Beginning** in reference to God does not refer to time. Since the Word was always with God, you can find no point of time at which he began to be but must necessarily admit his eternity. But here John means only that the devil had been an apostate since the creation of the world, and that from that time he had never ceased to scatter his poison among human beings.

The reason the Son of God appeared. John repeats in other words what he had said before, that Christ came to take away sins. Hence two conclusions are to be drawn: those in whom sin reigns cannot be reckoned among the members of Christ, and they can by no means belong to his body; for wherever Christ exerts his own power, he puts the devil to flight as well as sin. And this is what John immediately adds, for the next sentence, where he says that those who do not sin are born of God (verse 9), is a conclusion from what has gone before. It is an argument drawn from what is inconsistent, as I have already said, for the kingdom of Christ, which brings righteousness with it, cannot allow sin. But I have already said what not sinning means. The apostle does not make God's children wholly free from all sin; but he denies that any can really glory in this claim except those who strive from the heart to form their life in obedience to God.

The Pelagians and the Cathars made a wrong use of this passage when they imagined that the faithful are endued with angelic purity in this world; and some of the Anabaptists revived this idea. But all those who dream of a perfection of this kind show clearly enough what dull consciences they must have. The apostle's words are so far from countenancing their error that they are enough to rebut it.

9. No one who is born of God will continue to sin. Now, we must consider whether God wholly regenerates us at once or whether the remains of the old self continue in us until death. If regeneration is not as yet full and complete, it does not exempt us from the bondage of sin except in proportion to its own extent. Hence it appears that God's children cannot be free from sins and must sin every day, since they still have remnants of their old nature. Nevertheless, what the apostle argues stands unalterable—namely, that the purpose of regeneration is to destroy sin, and that all who are born of God lead a righteous and a holy life because the Spirit of God restrains the lusting of sin.

The apostle means the same thing by **God's seed**, for God's Spirit so forms the hearts of the godly for holy affections that the flesh and its lusts do not prevail, but being subdued and put as it were under a yoke, they are checked and restrained. In short, the apostle ascribes to the Spirit a sovereign presence in the elect; by his power he represses sin and does not allow it to rule and reign.

He cannot go on sinning. Here the apostle ascends higher, for he plainly declares that the hearts of the godly are so effectually governed by the Spirit of God that through an inflexible disposition they follow his guidance. Some theologians, while confessing that the human will cannot desire what is right unless assisted by God's Spirit, imagine such a motion of the Spirit as leaves us the free choice of good and evil. Hence they see merits because we willingly obey the influence of the Spirit, which it is in our power to resist. In short, they desire the grace of the Spirit to be only that we are thereby enabled to choose right if we will. John says something quite different here, for he not only shows that we cannot sin, but also that the power of the Spirit is so effectual that it necessarily keeps us in continual obedience to righteousness.

Nor is this the only passage of Scripture that teaches us that in Christ the will is so formed that it cannot be otherwise than right. For God testifies that he gives a new heart to his children and promises to do this so they may walk in his commandments. Besides, John not only shows how efficaciously God works in man but plainly says that the Spirit continues his grace in us to the last, so that inflexible perseverance is added to newness of life. Let us not, then, imagine that this is some neutral movement that leaves people free either to follow or to reject; but let us know that our own hearts are so ruled by God's Spirit that they constantly cling to righteousness.

Moreover, it is easy to refute the absurd argument of the Sophists that the will is taken away from us. They are wrong because the will is a natural power. But nature is corrupted; so the will only has depraved inclinations. Hence God's Spirit has to renew it in order that it may begin to be good.

And then, as we would immediately fall away from what is good, the same Spirit has to carry on to the end what he has begun.

As for merit, the answer is obvious, for it cannot be thought strange that people merit nothing; and yet good works, which flow from the grace of the Spirit, do not cease to be so deemed because they are voluntary. They also have a reward, for they are ascribed to us by grace, as though they were our own.

But here a question arises: Can the fear and love of God be extinguished in anyone who has been regenerated by the Spirit of God? The apostle's words seem to imply that this cannot be. Those who think otherwise refer to the example of David, who for a time labored under such a beastly stupor that not a spark of grace appeared in him. Moreover, in Psalm 51 he prays for the restoration of the Spirit; hence it follows that he was deprived of him. However, I do not doubt that the seed, communicated when God regenerates his chosen ones and being incorruptible, retains its goodness perpetually. Indeed, I grant that it may sometimes be stifled, as in the case of David; but still, when all religion seemed to be extinct in him, a live coal was hidden under the ashes. Satan, indeed, labors to root out whatever is from God in the elect; but when the utmost is permitted to him, there always remains a hidden root that springs up afterwards. But John is not speaking of one act, as people say, but of the continued course of life.

Some dream of something like an eternal seed in the elect that they bring from their mother's womb; but they most outrageously pervert John's words, for he is not speaking about eternal election but regeneration.

There are also those who are doubly mad, for they hold that everything is lawful for the faithful because John says they cannot sin. They maintain, then, that we may follow indiscriminately whatever our inclinations may lead us to. Thus they take the liberty to commit adultery, to steal, and to murder because there can be no sin where God's Spirit reigns. But the apostle's meaning is quite different. He denies that the faithful keep on sinning, because God has engraved his law on their hearts, as the prophet says (Jeremiah 31:33).

10. This is how we know who the children of God are. John sums up by concluding that it is wrong to claim a place and name among the children of God if we do not prove ourselves to be such by a pious and holy life, since this evidence shows that we differ from **the children of the devil.** But he does not mean that God's children are manifested in this way so that the whole world recognizes them. He only means that our fruit and adoption always appear in the way we live.

10b-13. Anyone who does not do what is right is not a child of God; neither is anyone who does not love his brother. This is the message you heard from the beginning: We should love one another. Do not be like Cain, who belonged to the evil one and murdered his brother. And why did he murder him? Because his own actions were evil and his brother's were righteous. Do not be surprised, my brothers, if the world hates you.

10. Anyone who does not do what is right. To do what is right and to sin are here set in opposition to each other. So then, to **do what is right** is nothing but to fear God from the heart and to walk in his commands as far as human weakness will permit; for though righteousness in a strict sense is a perfect keeping of the law, and the faithful are always far from this, offenses and falls are not imputed to them by God. So to **do what is right** means the imperfect obedience that they give him. But John says that everyone who does not do what is right is not of God, because all those whom God calls, he regenerates by his Spirit. Hence newness of life is a perpetual evidence of divine adoption.

Neither is anyone who does not love his brother. Earlier in the letter John has been exhorting the faithful to brotherly love; now he refers to true righteousness, adding this clause about love. I have already stated the reason why the whole of righteousness is included in brotherly love. The love of God, indeed, holds the first place; but as love for other people depends on it, it is often included in it. So then, the apostle is saying that everyone who is endued with benevolence and humanity is just and is to be regarded as such, because love is the fulfillment of the law. He confirms this declaration by saying that the faithful had been taught this **from the beginning** (verse 11). By these words he intimates that the statement he made should not have seemed new to them.

12. Do not be like Cain. This is another confirmation taken from an opposite: in the reprobate and the children of the devil, hatred reigns and holds the chief place in their life. John brings forward Cain as an example. This also serves to console his readers as he eventually concludes by saying, **Do not be surprised, my brothers, if the world hates you** (verse 13).

This explanation ought to be carefully noticed, for people are always blundering in regard to the way of life because they make holiness consist of fictitious works; and while they torment themselves with trifles, they think themselves doubly acceptable to God. But the apostle testifies that the only righteousness that is approved by God is if we love one another; and furthermore, the devil reigns where hatred, dissimulation, envy, and enmity prevail. However, we should also bear in mind what I have already touched upon—namely, that brotherly love, since it proceeds from the love of God just as an effect proceeds from a cause, is not disconnected from it, but on the contrary is commended by John because it is evidence of our love to God.

By saying that Cain was driven to kill his brother **because his own actions were evil**, John intimates what I have already stated: when impiety rules, hatred occupies the first place. He refers to Abel's righteous actions so that we may learn to endure patiently when the world hates us gratuitously, without any just provocation.

14-18. We know that we have passed from death to life, because we love our brothers. Anyone who does not love remains in death. Anyone who hates his brother is a murderer, and you know that no murderer has eternal life in him. This is how we know what love is: Jesus Christ laid down his life for us. And we ought to lay down our lives for our brothers. If anyone has material possessions and sees his brother in need but has no pity on him, how can the love of God be in him? Dear children, let us not love with words or tongue but with actions and in truth.

14. We know. John commends love to us with remarkable high praise, because it is evidence of his readers' transition from death to life. From this it follows that if we love the brothers, we are blessed, but that we are miserable if we hate them. There is no one who does not wish to be freed and delivered from death. So then, those who by cherishing hatred willingly give themselves up to death must be extremely stupid and senseless. But when the apostle says that love shows that we have passed into life, he does not mean that we are our own deliverers, as though by loving the brothers we could rescue ourselves from death and procure life for ourselves. He is not here dealing with the cause of salvation; rather, as love is the special fruit of the Spirit, it is also a sure symbol of regeneration.

So then, the apostle is drawing an argument from the sign, and not from the cause. For as no one sincerely loves his brothers unless he is regenerated by the Spirit of God, John rightly concludes that the Spirit of God, who is life, lives in all who love the brothers. But it would be preposterous for anyone to infer from this that life is obtained by love, since love comes afterwards chronologically.

The argument might seem more plausible if we said that love makes us more certain of life, for then confidence about salvation would rest on works. But the answer to this is obvious. Though faith is confirmed by all the graces of God as aids, it does not cease to have its foundation in God's mercy alone. For instance, when we enjoy the light, we are certain that the sun is shining; if the sun shines on the place where we are, we have a clearer view of it. But when the rays of light do not reach us, we are still satisfied that the sun diffuses its light for our benefit. Similarly, when faith is founded on Christ, some things may happen to assist it, but it still rests on Christ's grace alone.

15. Is a murderer. To stimulate us still more to love, John shows how detestable hatred is to God. There is no one who does not dread a murderer; we all execrate the very word. But the apostle declares that all who hate their brothers are murderers. He could have said nothing more atrocious; nor is what he says hyperbolical, for those we hate, we wish to perish. It does not matter if we keep our hands from mischief; the very desire to do harm, as well as the attempt, is condemned before God. Indeed, when we do not ourselves seek to do an injury but wish an evil to happen to our brother from someone else, we are murderers.

So then, the apostle defines the thing simply as it is when he ascribes murder to hatred. This proves the folly of people who pay no attention to the crime itself while they abominate the word. Why is this? It is because the external face of things engrosses our thoughts; but the inward feeling is called to account before God. Let no one, therefore, extenuate any longer such a grievous evil. Let us learn to refer our judgments to God's tribunal.

16. This is how we know what true love is. It would not have been enough to commend love unless its power was understood. As an instance of perfect love, John sets before us the example of Christ. By not sparing his own life, Christ testified how much he loved us. This, then, is the goal toward which the apostle calls them to advance. To sum up, our love is approved when we transfer the love of ourselves to our brothers, so that each of us, as we forget ourselves, seeks the good of others.

It is, indeed, certain that we are far from being equal to Christ; but the apostle calls us to imitate him. Though we will not overtake him, it is still right for us to follow his steps, even at a distance. It was the apostle's aim to beat down the vain boasting of hypocrites who gloried that they had faith in Christ without brotherly love. Therefore, his words doubtless mean that unless this feeling prevails in our hearts, we have no connection with Christ. And as I have said before, he does not set the love of Christ before us so as to require us to be equal to him; for what would this be but to drive us all to despair? He means that our feelings should be so formed and regulated that we may desire to devote our life, and also our death, first to God and then to our neighbors.

There is another difference between us and Christ: the virtue or benefit of our death cannot be the same. For the wrath of God is not pacified by our blood, nor is life procured by our death, nor is the punishment that others deserve suffered by us. But the apostle, in this comparison, was not thinking about the end of the effect of Christ's death; he meant only that our life should conform to his example.

17. If anyone has material possessions. John speaks now about the common duties of love, which flow from a foundation of being prepared to serve our neighbors even to the point of giving our lives for them. The apostle seems to be reasoning from the less to the greater, for anyone who refuses to use his own property to alleviate his brother's needs while his own life is safe and secure would be far less likely to put his own life in danger for him. So John denies that there is love in us if we withhold help from our neighbors. But in recommending this external kindness, he rightly expresses the proper way of doing good and the sort of feeling we ought to have.

Let this be the first proposition, then: no one truly loves his brothers if he does not show this whenever an opportunity occurs. The second is that a person must help his brothers as much as he is able, for the Lord gives us opportunity to exercise love in this way. The third is that each person's need should be attended to, for anyone who needs food and drink, or other things that we have plenty of, requires our help. The fourth is that no act of kindness pleases God unless it is accompanied with sympathy. There are many apparently generous people who do not feel for the miseries of their brothers. But the apostle requires that we have **pity**, which happens when we feel sympathy with others in their distress just as if it were our own.

The love of God. Here John speaks of loving the brothers. Why, then, does he mention the love of God? It is because of the principle that the love of God necessarily generates love of the brothers in us. God tests our love to him when he calls us to love people out of regard for himself.

18. Let us not love with words or tongue. We cannot love only with words or tongue; but since many people falsely claim this, the apostle lets the name of the thing be used for their pretended love, although in the second clause he reproves them by denying that there is reality except in the deed. So the words must be explained like this: "Let us not profess with our tongues that we love, but prove it by the deed, for this is the only true way of showing love."

19-22. This then is how we know that we belong to the truth, and how we set our hearts at rest in his presence whenever our hearts condemn us. For God is greater than our hearts, and he knows everything. Dear friends, if our hearts do not condemn us, we have confidence before God and receive from him anything we ask, because we obey his commands and do what pleases him

19. This then is how we know. John now takes the word **truth** in a different sense; but there is a striking similarity with the previous meaning. If we in truth love our neighbors, we have evidence that we are born of God, who is truth, or that the truth of God lives in us. But we must always remember that it is not from love that we get the knowledge the apostle mentions, as though we were looking to it for the certainty of salvation. Doubtless there is no other way we know that we are God's children except by his sealing his free adoption in our hearts by his own Spirit and by our receiving by faith the sure pledge of it offered in Christ. Thus love is an accessory or a prop to our faith, not a foundation on which it rests.

Why, then, does the apostle say, **We have confidence before God** (verse 21)? In these words he is reminding us that faith does not exist without a good conscience; it is not that assurance arises from it or depends on it, but that we are only really (and not falsely) assured of our union with God when he manifests himself in our love by the working of his Holy Spirit. It is always right and proper to consider what the apostle is dealing with; even as he condemns a false profession of faith, he says that we cannot have a genuine assurance before God unless his Spirit produces the fruit of love in us. Nevertheless, though a good conscience cannot be separated from faith, no one should conclude from this that we must look to our works to make our conscience certain.

20. Whenever our hearts condemn us. The apostle proves, on the other hand, that it is useless for people to be called Christians if they do not have the testimony of a good conscience, for if anyone is conscious of guilt and is condemned by his own heart, much less can he escape God's judgment. Hence it follows that faith is subverted by the disquiet of an evil conscience.

God is greater than our hearts. This refers to judgment; that is, God sees much more keenly than we do and searches more minutely and judges more severely. For this reason Paul says that though he was not conscious of wrong in himself, that did not mean he was justified (1 Corinthians 4:4), for he knew that however carefully he attended to his duty, he went wrong in many ways and through inadvertence was ignorant of mistakes that God perceived. What the apostle means, then, is that someone who is harassed and condemned by his own conscience cannot escape God's judgment.

What comes next says the same thing: God **knows** or sees **everything**. How can anything be hidden from him when we who are dull and blind in comparison with him see it? So the words should be explained thus: "Since God sees everything, he is far superior to our hearts." The meaning is now clear: since the knowledge of God penetrates deeper than the perceptions of our conscience, no one can stand before him unless the integrity of his conscience sustains him.

But here a question may be raised. It is certain that the reprobate are sometimes sunk by Satan into such stupor that they are no longer conscious of their own evils and, as Paul says, fearlessly rush into perdition; it is also certain that hypocrites usually flatter themselves and proudly disregard God's judgment, for they are drunk on false conceit about their own righteousness and feel no conviction of sin. The answer to these things is not difficult. Hypocrites are deceived because they shun the light, and the reprobate feel nothing because they have departed from God; indeed, there is no security for an evil conscience but in hiding-places.

But the apostle is speaking here about consciences that God draws into the light, forces to his tribunal, and fills with an awareness of his judgment. Yet it is at the same time generally true that we cannot have a calm peace apart from that which God's Spirit gives to purified hearts. Those who are stupefied, as we have said, often feel secret compunctions and torment themselves in their lethargy.

21. If our hearts do not condemn us. I have already explained that this refers not to hypocrites nor to the gross despisers of God. For however satisfied the reprobate may be with their own lives, the Lord weighs their motives (Proverbs 16:2). No one can boast of having a clean heart. So the apostle's words mean that we can only come into God's presence in calm confidence when we bring with us the testimony of a heart that is conscious of what is right and honest. Paul's saying is indeed true—that confident access to God is opened to us by faith, which relies on the grace of Christ (Ephesians 3:12). Also, peace is given to us by faith, so that our conscience may stand peaceably before God (Romans 5:1). Paul shows the cause of confidence, while John mentions only an inseparable addition— something that necessarily accompanies it, though it is not the cause.

Here, however, arises a greater difficulty, which seems to leave no confidence in the whole world; for who can be found who does not feel guilty about something? To this I answer that godly people are reproved in this way but may at the same time be absolved. It is indeed necessary for them to be seriously troubled inwardly for their sins, so that terror may lead them to humility and to a hatred of themselves; but they soon flee to the sacrifice of Christ, where they are sure of peace. Yet in another sense the apostle says they are not condemned, because however deficient they may confess themselves to be in many things, they are still relieved by this testimony of conscience, so that they truly and from the heart fear God and desire to submit to his righteousness. All who possess this godly feeling and at the same time know that all their endeavors, however far they may come short of perfection, still please God are rightly said to have a calm or a peaceful heart, because there is no inward compunction to disturb their calm cheerfulness.

22. Anything we ask. Confidence and prayer are connected. John has already shown that a bad conscience is inconsistent with confidence, and now he says that no one can really pray to God except those who fear and worship him properly—that is, with a pure heart. The one follows from the other. It is a general truth taught in Scripture that God does not listen to the ungodly, but that, on the contrary, their sacrifices and prayers are abominations to him. Hence the door is shut to hypocrites, lest they rush into his presence in contempt of him.

Still, John does not mean that a good conscience must be brought, as though it obtained favor for our prayers. Woe to us if we rely on works, which have nothing in them but cause to fear and tremble. The faithful, then, cannot come to God's tribunal except by relying on Christ the Mediator. But as the love of God is always linked with faith, the apostle severely reproves hypocrites by depriving them of that unique privilege with which God favors his own children, lest they should think their prayers can reach God.

Because we obey his commands. John does not mean that confidence in prayer is based on our works; he is only teaching that true religion and the sincere worship of God cannot be separated from faith. Nor should it seem strange that he uses the word **because,** for an inseparable addition is sometimes mentioned as a cause.

23-24. And this is his command: to believe in the name of his Son, Jesus Christ, and to love one another as he commanded us. Those who obey his commands live in him, and he in them. And this is how we know that he lives in us: We know it by the Spirit he gave us.

23. And this is his command. Again John uses a general truth for a specific purpose. The meaning is that such is the discord between us and God that we are kept away from him unless we are united to one another by love. At the same time the apostle is not here commending love alone, as before, but as the companion and attendant of faith.

The Sophists by their misinterpretations distort these words, as though liberty to pray were obtained by us partly by faith and partly by works. As John requires us to keep God's commands so that we may pray properly and afterwards teaches us that this keeping of his command refers to faith and love, they conclude that we ought to derive confidence in prayer from these two things. But I have already reminded you several times that the subject here is not how or by what means people may prepare themselves so that they may have confidence to pray to God, for John is not here speaking about the cause of this or of any worthiness. He is only showing that God favors none but his own children with the honor and privilege of fellowship with himself; it is only for those who have been regenerated by his Spirit. The meaning of what he says, then, is that where the fear and love of God do not prevail, it cannot be that God will hear prayer.

But if we want to obey his commands, let us see what he tells us to do. He does not separate faith from love but requires both from us.

This is a remarkable passage, for John defines briefly as well as lucidly what it is that makes the perfection of a holy life. There is no reason for us to have any difficulty about it, since God does not by any means lead us through long labyrinths, but simply and shortly sets before us what is right and what he approves of. Besides, there is nothing obscure about this brevity, for he clearly shows us the beginning and the end of a life rightly shaped. Why does John only mention brotherly love here and omit the love of God? The reason, as we have said elsewhere, is that brotherly love flows from the love of God, and so it is a sure and real evidence of it.

In the name of his Son. The name refers to preaching, and this link deserves to be noticed, for few people understand what it is to believe in Christ. From this manner of speaking we may easily see that the only true faith is that which embraces Christ as he is set forth in the Gospel. That is why there is no faith without preaching, as Paul also shows us in Romans 10:14. We must also notice that the apostles included faith in the knowledge of Christ; for he is the living image of the Father, and in him are stored up all the treasures of wisdom and knowledge. As soon as we turn aside from him, we cannot do anything but wander in error.

24. Those who obey his commands. John now confirms what I have already said, that the union we have with God is evident when we entertain mutual love—not that our union begins by it, but that it cannot be fruitless or without effect whenever it begins to exist. And he proves this by adding a reason: because God does not remain in us unless his Spirit lives in us. And wherever the Spirit is, he necessarily reveals his power and efficacy. Hence we may readily conclude that the only people who remain in God and are united to him are those who keep his commands.

And this is how we know. The word **and** should be translated "for" or "because." The nature of the reason being given ought to be considered; for though the words agree with those of Paul when he says that the Spirit testifies to our hearts that we are the children of God, and that through him we cry "*Abba*, Father," there is some difference in the sense. Paul is speaking about the certainty of free adoption, which the Spirit of God seals on our hearts. But here John is thinking about the effects that the Spirit produces while living in us, as Paul himself does when he says that people who are led by the Spirit of God are God's children. There also he is speaking about the mortification of the flesh and newness of life.

The sum of what is said is that when God's Spirit rules and governs our life, we are clearly seen to be his children. John also teaches us that whatever good works are done by us proceed from the grace of the Spirit and that the Spirit is not obtained by our righteousness, but is freely given to us.

Chapter 4

1-3. Dear friends, do not believe every spirit, but test the spirits to see whether they are from God, because many false prophets have gone out into the world. This is how you can recognize the Spirit of God: Every spirit that acknowledges that Jesus Christ has come in the flesh is from God, but every spirit that does not acknowledge Jesus is not from God. This is the spirit of the antichrist, which you have heard is coming and even now is already in the world.

John returns to his earlier doctrine, which he had touched upon in the second chapter. As is usual with anything new, many people had abused the name of Christ for the purpose of serving their own errors. Some people made a half-profession of Christ; and when they obtained a place among his friends, they had more opportunity to injure his cause. Satan used this opportunity to disturb the church, especially regarding Christ himself, for he is the stumbling block against whom everybody must stumble who does not keep on the right way, as shown to us by God.

What the apostle says consists of three parts. First, he points to an evil that is dangerous to the faithful, and therefore he urges them to beware. He prescribes how they were to beware—that is, by making a distinction between the spirits; and this is the second part. In the third place, he points out a particular error, the most dangerous to them; he therefore forbids them to listen to those who denied that the Son of God had appeared in the flesh. We shall now consider each of these in order.

The passage adds that **many false prophets have gone out into the world,** and it is convenient to begin with this. This announcement contains a useful admonition, for if Satan had already seduced many people who, under the name of Christ, spread their errors around, then similar instances today need not terrify us. It is always the case with the Gospel that Satan attempts to pollute and corrupt its purity by a variety of errors. Our own age has brought forth some horrible and monstrous sects, and for this reason many people are confused and, not knowing where to turn, cast off all thought for religion because they cannot find any quicker way to extricate themselves from the danger of errors. Such a course is most foolish, for by shunning the light of truth they cast themselves into the darkness of errors. Therefore, let this fact remain fixed in our minds, that from the time the Gospel began to be preached, false prophets immediately appeared; this fact will strengthen us against such offenses.

The antiquity of errors keeps many people firmly tied up, as it were, so that they dare not emerge from them. But here John points out an internal evil that was then in the church. If there were impostors mixed with the apostles and other faithful teachers then, what wonder is it that the doctrine of the Gospel has been suppressed for a long time and that many corruptions have prevailed in the world? There is, then, no reason why we should not exercise our liberty in distinguishing between truth and falsehood even though the errors are long established.

1. Do not believe every spirit. When the church is disturbed by discord and contention, many people are frightened and depart from the Gospel. But the Spirit prescribes to us a very different remedy: the faithful should not accept any doctrine without thought or discrimination. We ought, then, to take heed lest, being offended at the variety of opinions, we should discard teachers and, together with them, the Word of God. But it is sufficient precaution if we do not listen indiscriminately to every teacher.

I take the word **spirit** to mean someone who boasts that he is endowed with the gift of the Spirit to perform his office as a prophet. It was not permitted for anyone to speak in his own name, nor was credit given to speakers except insofar as they were the organs of the Holy Spirit, in order that prophets might have more authority. God honored them with his name as though he had separated them from mankind in general. So then, the people who were called "spirits" were those who represented the Holy Spirit by putting his oracles into words. They brought nothing of their own, nor did they speak on their own authority. But the point of this honorable title was that God's Word should not lose the respect due to it through the humble condition of the minister. For God wanted his Word always to be received from human mouths just as if he himself had appeared from heaven.

Here Satan interposed, sending false teachers to adulterate God's Word and giving them this title, so that they might deceive people more easily. Thus false prophets have always boldly claimed for themselves whatever honor God had bestowed on his own servants. But the apostle deliberately made use of this name, lest those who falsely claim God's authority should deceive us by their masks.

We ought therefore to note that the apostle might have said that not every sort of person ought to be believed; but false teachers claimed the Spirit, and he did not challenge that claim directly. At the same time, he reminded people that those teachers' claim was frivolous and invalid if they did not exhibit what they professed. It was foolish for anyone to be over-awed by the mere sound of such an honorable name without daring to make any inquiry on the subject.

Test the spirits. As all were not true prophets, the apostle here declares that they ought to be examined and tested. And he addresses not just the whole church, but every individual believer.

You may ask where this discernment is to be obtained. Those who answer that the Word of God is the rule by which everything that people bring forward ought to be tested are giving some of the answer, but not the whole. I accept that doctrines ought to be tested by God's Word, but unless the Spirit of wisdom is present, having God's Word in our hands will avail little or nothing, for its meaning will not be apparent to us. In the same way, gold is tested by fire or a touchstone, but this can only be done by those who understand how to do it, for neither the touchstone nor fire can be of any use to anyone who does not have the skill. If we are to be fit to judge, we must allow the Spirit of discernment to direct us. It would have been in vain for the apostle to command this if no power of judging were supplied; so we may conclude with certainty that godly people will never be left without the Spirit of wisdom to show them what is necessary, provided they ask the Lord for his assistance. But the Spirit will only thus guide us to a correct discrimination when we make all our thoughts subject to God's Word; for as I said, like a touchstone, the Word should be regarded as most necessary to us, for only true doctrine is drawn from it.

But here a difficult question arises: If everyone has the right and the liberty to judge, nothing can be settled as certain, but on the contrary the whole of religion will be uncertain. My answer to this is that there is a double test of doctrine—private and public. The private test is that by which everyone settles his own faith, relying wholly on the doctrine that is known to come from God; for consciences will never find a safe and tranquil haven other than in God. The public test is the common consent and polity of the church; for as there is a danger of fanatics arising who may presume to boast that they are endued with God's Spirit, it is necessary for the faithful to meet together and seek a way by which they may agree in a holy and godly manner. The old proverb is too true: "So many heads, so many opinions"; and it is doubtless God's unique task to subdue our perverseness and make us think the same thing and agree in a holy unity of faith.

The idea that whatever has been decreed in councils is to be regarded as certain, because the church has proved the doctrine to be from God, is extremely frivolous. Although the usual way of seeking consent is to convene a godly and holy council at which controversies may be decided according to God's Word, God has never bound himself to the decrees of any council. Nor does it necessarily follow that as soon as a hundred bishops or more meet together in any place, they have duly called on God and inquired of him what is true. Indeed, nothing is more clear than that they have often departed from the pure Word of God. So then, in this case also the trial prescribed by the apostle ought to take place, so that the spirits may be tested.

2. This is how you can recognize the Spirit of God. John lays down a special mark by which they might more easily distinguish between true and false prophets. Yet he only repeats here what we have already come across: just as Christ is the object at which faith aims, so also he is the stone on which all heretics stumble. As long as we remain in Christ, then, we are safe; but when we depart from him, faith is lost, and all truth is invalidated.

But let us consider what this confession includes, for when the apostle says that Christ **has come**, we conclude that he had previously been with the Father. This proves his eternal divinity. By saying that he has come **in the flesh,** John means that by putting on flesh Christ became a real man, with the same nature as we have, so that he might become our brother, except that he was free from every sin and corruption. And lastly, by saying that he **has come,** the cause of his coming must be noticed, for it was not for nothing that he was sent by the Father. So the office and merits of Christ depend on this.

The heretics in olden times departed from the faith, in one case by deny-ing the divine nature of Christ, and in another case by denying his human nature. People who confess Christ to be God and man are still departing from the faith if they do not adhere to the confession that the apostle requires, because they rob Christ of his own merit. Where free will, merits of works, fictitious modes of worship, satisfactions, and the advocacy of saints are set up, how very little remains for Christ!

The apostle, then, meant that since the knowledge of Christ includes the sum and substance of the doctrine concerning true religion, we ought to fix our eyes on that so that we may not be deceived. Doubtless Christ is the end of the law and the prophets; nor do we learn anything else from the Gospel but his power and grace.

3. This is the spirit of the antichrist. The apostle adds this to make us detest all the more any errors that lead us away from Christ. We have already said that the doctrine concerning the kingdom of Antichrist was well-known, and the faithful had been warned about the future scattering of the church so that they might watch out. It was right, then, for them to dread the name as something base and ominous. The apostle now says that all those who reduced Christ were members of that kingdom.

And he says that **the spirit of the antichrist** would come, and that **even now** it **is already in the world**, but in a different sense. He means that it was already in the world because it carried on its evil work in secret. As, however, the truth of God had not as yet been subverted by false and spu-rious dogmas, as superstition had not as yet prevailed in corrupting the worship of God, as the world had not as yet departed from Christ, as tyranny, opposed to the kingdom of Christ, had not as yet openly exalted itself, he says that it was still to come.

4-6. You, dear children, are from God and have overcome them, because the one who is in you is greater than the one who is in the world. They are from the world and therefore speak from the viewpoint of the world, and the world listens to them. We are from God, and whoever knows God listens to us; but whoever is not from God does not listen to us. This is how we recognize the spirit of truth and the spirit of falsehood.

4. You ... are from God. John had spoken about one antichrist; now he mentions many (**them**). But the many were the false prophets who had appeared before the head appeared. The apostle wanted to inspire the faith-ful to resist impostors courageously and boldly, for we are not too eager when the outcome of the contest is in doubt. Besides, it might have caused good people to be afraid when they saw that the kingdom of Christ had hardly been set up and enemies were ready to suppress it. So he says that although they must fight, they have conquered, because they will win. This is like saying that even in the middle of the battle they were already beyond danger, because they would certainly be conquerors.

But this truth ought to be extended further, for whatever battles we may have with the world and the flesh, certain victory is to follow. Hard and fierce conflicts indeed await us, and some continually succeed others; but as by Christ's power we fight and are furnished with God's weapons, we become conquerors just by fighting and striving. As for the main subject of this passage, it is a great consolation that however Satan attacks us, we shall stand through God's power.

But we must notice the reason that is immediately added: **because the one who is in you is greater than the one who is in the world.** Such is our weakness that we succumb before we engage an enemy, for we are so ignorant that we are open to all kinds of fallacies, and Satan is wonderfully artful in deception. If we were to hold out for one day, a doubt may creep into our minds as to what would happen tomorrow; we should thus be in a state of perpetual anxiety. Therefore, the apostle reminds us that we become strong not by our own power but by that of God. From this he concludes that we cannot be conquered any more than God himself, who has armed us with his own power to the end of the world. But in this whole spiritual warfare this thought should dwell in our hearts: it would be all over with us immediately were we to fight in our own strength, but as God repels our enemies while we are resting, victory is certain.

5. They are from the world. It is no small consolation that those who dare to assail God in us have only the world to aid and help them. By **the world** the apostle means that portion of which Satan is the prince. Another consolation is also added when he says that the world embraces through the false prophets what it acknowledges as its own. We see how prone people are to vanity and falsehood. Hence false doctrines easily penetrate and spread far and wide. The apostle says there is no reason for us to be disturbed because of this, for it is nothing new or unusual that the world, which is wholly fallacious, should readily listen to what is false.

6. We are from God. Though this really applies to all godly people, it refers strictly to the faithful ministers of the Gospel; for here the apostle, with the confidence imparted by the Spirit, is glorying that he and his fellow ministers served God in sincerity and derived from him whatever they taught. It happens that false prophets boast of the same thing, for it is their custom to deceive under the mask of God. But faithful ministers are quite different from them, because they only declare what is really manifest in their conduct.

However, we should always bear in mind the subject that the apostle is dealing with here. The number of godly people was small, and unbelief prevailed almost everywhere. Few people really adhered to the Gospel; most were running headlong into error. This was the cause of stumbling. In order to obviate this, John tells us to be content with the small number of the faithful, because all God's children honor him and submit to his doctrine. John immediately sets in opposition to this the fact that **whoever is not from God does not listen** to the pure doctrine of the Gospel. Thus he is saying that the vast multitude, to whom the Gospel is not acceptable, do not listen to the faithful and true servants of God because they are alienated from God himself. It does not lessen the authority of the Gospel, then, that many people reject it.

There is a useful warning added to this doctrine. By the obedience of faith we are to prove ourselves to be from God. It is easy to boast that we are from God, and so nothing is more common among us. People proudly boast that they worship God, and yet they no less proudly reject God's Word. Or they pretend to believe God's Word, and yet when they are brought to the test they close their ears and will not listen. But to revere God's Word is the only true evidence that we fear him. Nor can the excuse made by many people have any place here, that they shun the doctrine of the Gospel when it is proclaimed to them because they are not fit to form a judgment. Everyone who really fears and obeys God must know him in his Word.

If anyone objects that many of the chosen people do not immediately attain faith and at first resist it stubbornly, I answer that we should not at that time regard them as God's children, for it is the sign of a reprobate person to reject the truth perversely.

And by the way, notice that the listening mentioned by the apostle is to be understood of the inward and real listening of the heart, which is done by faith.

This is how we recognize. The word **this** refers to the two preceding clauses. This is like saying, "The truth is distinguished from falsehood because some people speak from God, others from the world."

The spirit [NIV margin] **of truth and the spirit of falsehood.** Some people think this means listeners, as though John said that those who give themselves up to be deceived by impostors were born to error and had the seed of falsehood in them, but that those who obey the Word of God show themselves by this very fact to be the children of the truth. I do not agree with this view, for the apostle uses the word *spirit* in this section to mean a teacher or prophet, and I think he means simply that the test of doctrine must be whether it comes from God or from the world.

However, by speaking in this way he seems to be saying nothing; for everyone is able to say that they speak only from God. But to all this I reply that we have the Word of the Lord, which ought especially to be consulted. When, therefore, false spirits claim to speak in God's name, we must inquire from the Scriptures whether this is so. Provided a devout attention is exercised, accompanied with humility and meekness, the spirit of discernment will be given to us, and as a faithful interpreter God will reveal to us the meaning of what is said in Scripture.

7-10. Dear friends, let us love one another, for love comes from God. Everyone who loves has been born of God and knows God. Whoever does not love does not know God, because God is love. This is how God showed his love among us: He sent his one and only Son into the world that we might live through him. This is love: not that we loved God, but that he loved us and sent his Son as an atoning sacrifice for our sins.

7. Dear friends. John returns to the exhortation that he reinforces throughout almost the entire letter. We have, indeed, said that it is filled with the doctrine of faith and the exhortation to love. On these two points the apostle lingers so much that he continually passes from the one to the other.

Let us love one another. He does not mean that we discharge this duty when we love our friends, because they love us; but as he is speaking to all the faithful together, he had to say that they were to exercise mutual love. He confirms this sentence by a reason often adduced before—namely, that no one can prove himself to be a child of God without loving his neighbors; the true knowledge of God necessarily produces love in us.

He also sets in opposition to this, as is his custom, the contrary clause: there is no knowledge of God when there is no love (verse 8). And he takes for granted a general principle or truth: God is love—that is, it is his nature to love us. I know that many people offer more complicated interpretations and that the ancient writers especially perverted this passage in order to prove the divinity of the Spirit. But the apostle simply means that as God is the fountain of love, this effect flows from him and is diffused wherever the knowledge of him comes, just as John had started the letter by calling God light because there is nothing dark in him, but on the contrary he illuminates everything by his own brightness. Here, then, John is not speaking about God's essence but is showing what we find him to be.

But two things in the apostle's words should be noticed: the true knowledge of God is that which regenerates and renews us, so that we become new creatures; and we must therefore necessarily conform to the image of God. Away with that foolish interpretation, then, about unformed faith. When anyone separates faith from love, it is as if he attempted to take away heat from the sun.

9. This is how God showed his love among us. The love of God toward us is testified also by many other proofs. If you ask why the world has been created, why we have been placed in it to rule over the earth, why we are preserved in life to enjoy innumerable blessings, why we are endued with light and understanding, no other reason can be given except the free love of God. But the apostle here has chosen the principal evidence of it, that which far surpasses everything else. It was not only an immeasurable love that God did not spare his own Son, that by his death he might restore us to life; it was also the most marvelous goodness, which should fill our minds with the greatest wonder and amazement. Christ, then, is so illustrious and remarkable a proof of divine love toward us that whenever we look at him, he fully confirms the truth that God is love.

His one and only Son. John calls him this for the sake of amplification. This shows more clearly how singularly God loved us when he exposed his only Son to death for our sakes. He who is his only Son by nature makes many sons by grace and adoption—all who, by faith, are united to his body. The apostle expresses the purpose for which Christ has been sent by the Father—namely, that we may live through him, for without him we are all dead; but by his coming he brought life to us, and unless our unbelief prevents the effect of his grace, we feel it in ourselves.

10. This is love. He amplifies God's love by another reason: he gave us his own Son at the time when we were enemies, as Paul teaches us in Romans 5:8. But John uses different words, saying that God, induced by no love of ours, freely loved us. By these words John means to teach us that God's love toward us has been gratuitous. And though it was the apostle's aim to show how God is an example to be imitated by us, the doctrine of faith that he mixes with it should not be overlooked. God freely loved us. How so? Because he loved us before we were born, and also when, through natural depravity, we had hearts turned away from him and were influenced by no right and pious feelings.

Some people have thought that everyone is chosen by God according to whether he foresees them to be worthy of love. If this were the case, the doctrine that he loved us first would not stand; for then our love to God would come first, though chronologically later. But the apostle assumes it as an evident truth, taught in Scripture, that we are born so corrupt and depraved that there is a sort of innate hatred to God born in us, so that we desire nothing but what is displeasing to him, and all the passions of our flesh continually war against his righteousness.

And sent his Son. So then, it was from God's goodness alone, as from a fountain, that Christ with all his blessings has come to us. And just as we need to know that we have salvation in Christ because our heavenly Father has freely loved us, so when a real and full certainty of divine love to us is sought for, we must look only to Christ. Hence it is mad to inquire, apart from Christ, what is settled concerning us in God's secret counsel.

As an atoning sacrifice for our sins. Again John points out the cause of Christ's coming and his function. First, indeed, we are taught by these words that through sin we were all alienated from God, and that this alienation and discord remains until Christ intervenes to reconcile us. Second, we are taught that the beginning of our life is when God, having been pacified by the death of his Son, receives us into favor, for **atoning sacrifice** refers to the sacrifice of Christ's death. We find, then, that this honor of expiating for the sins of the world, thus taking away the enmity between God and us, belongs only to Christ.

But here there seems to be some inconsistency, for if God loved us before Christ offered himself to die for us, what need was there for another reconciliation? In this way the death of Christ may seem to be superfluous. To this I answer that when it says that Christ reconciled the Father to us, it refers to our apprehension, for as we are conscious of being guilty, we cannot conceive of God except as one displeased and angry with us, until Christ absolves us from guilt. Wherever sin appears, God wants his wrath and the judgment of eternal death to be stopped. Hence it follows that we can only be terrified by the present prospect concerning death until Christ by his death abolishes sin, until he delivers us by his own blood from death. Further, God's love requires righteousness; so if we are to be persuaded that we are loved, we have to come to Christ, in whom alone is righteousness to be found.

We now see that the variety of expressions that occurs in Scripture is most appropriate and especially useful with regard to faith. God interposed his own Son to reconcile himself to us, because he loved us; but this love was hidden, because we were enemies of God, continually provoking his wrath. Besides, the fear and terror of an evil conscience took away from us all enjoyment of life. Hence, as it seemed to the awareness of our faith, God began to love us in Christ. Though the apostle here speaks about the first reconciliation, let us be sure that making God propitious toward us by expiating our sins is a perpetual benefit coming from Christ.

11-16. Dear friends, since God so loved us, we also ought to love one another. No one has ever seen God; but if we love each other, God lives in us and his love is made complete in us. We know that we live in him and he in us, because he has given us of his Spirit. And we have seen and testify that the Father has sent his Son to be the Savior of the world. If anyone acknowledges that Jesus is the Son of God, God lives in him and he in God. And so we know and rely on the love God has for us. God is love. Whoever lives in love lives in God, and God in him.

11. Dear friends. The apostle now accommodates to his own purpose what he has just taught us about the love of God, for he urges us by God's example to **love one another.** Paul, too, sets Christ before us as offering himself to the Father as a fragrant sacrifice so that each of us might labor to benefit our neighbors (Ephesians 5:2). And John reminds us that our love ought not to be mercenary. He tells us to love our neighbors as **God so loved us,** for we ought to remember that we have been loved freely. And doubtless when we think about our own advantage or do good things for our friends, it is self-love, and not love to others.

12. No one has ever seen God. The same words are found in the first chapter of John's Gospel (1:18); but there John the Baptist was not thinking of exactly the same thing, for he meant only that God could only be known as he has revealed himself in Christ. Here the apostle extends the same truth further, showing that the power of God is comprehended by us by faith and love, so that we know that we are his children and that he dwells in us.

However, the apostle speaks first of love when he says that **God lives in** us if we love one another, for his love is **made complete** or really proved to be in us then. This is like saying that God shows himself as present when by his Spirit he forms our hearts so that they maintain brotherly love. For the same purpose he repeats what he had already said, that we know by the Spirit whom he has given us that he lives in us; this is a confirmation of the previous sentence, because love is the effect or fruit of the Spirit.

To sum up what has been said, since love comes from the Spirit of God, we cannot truly and with a sincere heart love one another unless the Spirit gives us his power. In this way he testifies that he lives in us. God lives in us by his Spirit; so then, by love we prove that we have God remaining in us. On the other hand, whoever boasts that he has God and does not love his brothers, his falsehood is proved by that one thing, because he separates God from himself.

And his love is made complete in us. The word **and** should be taken as a causative—"for," "because." And **love** here may be explained in two ways—either that which God shows to us, or that which he implants in us. That God has given his Spirit to us, or has given us of his Spirit, means the same thing, for we know that the Spirit in a measure is given to each individual.

14. And we have seen. John now explains the other part of the knowledge of God, which we have referred to—that he communicates himself to us in his Son and offers himself to be enjoyed through him. It follows from this that Christ is received by us by faith, for the apostle's purpose is to show that God is so united to us by faith and love that he really lives in us and makes himself in a sense visible by the effect of his power, when otherwise he could not be seen by us.

When the apostle says, **we have seen and testify**, he is referring to himself and others. By seeing he does not mean just any sort of seeing, but that which belongs to faith, by which they recognized the glory of God in Christ, according to what follows—namely, that he was **sent . . . to be the Savior of the world.** This knowledge flows from the illumination of the Spirit.

15. If anyone acknowledges. John repeats the truth that we are united to God by Christ and that we cannot be connected with Christ unless God remains in us. Acknowledgment means the same as faith, for though hypocrites boast falsely of faith, the apostle here means only those who believe truly and from the heart. Besides, when he says that **Jesus is the Son of**

God, he includes in this brief statement the sum and substance of faith, for nothing is necessary for salvation that faith does not find in Christ.

Having said in general that people are so united to Christ by faith that Christ unites them to God, he adds what they themselves had seen. He accommodates a general truth to those to whom he was writing. Then follows the exhortation to love one another as they were loved by God. Therefore, the order and logic of his discourse is this: Faith in Christ makes God live in us, and we share in this grace; but as God is love, no one lives in him without loving the brothers. So then, love ought to reign in us since God unites himself to us.

16. And so we know and rely on the love God has for us. This is the same as saying, "We have known by believing," for such knowledge is only attained by faith. But from this we learn how different faith is from an uncertain or doubtful opinion. Besides, though as I have said he meant here to accommodate the last sentence to his readers, the apostle still defines faith in various ways. He had already said that it is to acknowledge that Jesus is the Son of God; now he says that by faith we know God's love toward us. From this we see that God's fatherly love is found in Christ and that nothing certain is known of Christ except by those who know themselves to be the children of God by his grace. For the Father sets his own Son before us each day in order that he may adopt us in him.

God is love. This is as it were the minor proposition in an argument, for he reasons from faith to love in this way: By faith God lives in us, and **God is love;** therefore, wherever God remains, love ought to be there. Hence it follows that love is necessarily connected with faith.

17-18. Love is made complete among us so that we will have confidence on the day of judgment, because in this world we are like him. There is no fear in love. But perfect love drives out fear, because fear has to do with punishment. The one who fears is not made perfect in love.

17. Love is made complete among us. There are two clauses in this passage—that we share divine adoption when we resemble God in the same way that children resemble their father; and, second, this **confidence** is invaluable, for without it we must be most miserable.

In the first place, he shows why God has embraced us in love and how we enjoy that grace revealed to us in Christ. God's love to us is what is to be understood here. He says it is **made complete** because it is poured out abundantly and is truly given, so that it appears to be complete. But he asserts that the only people who share this blessing are those who, by being conformed to God, prove themselves to be his children. This is, then, an argument from what is an inseparable condition.

So that we will have confidence. He now begins to show the fruit of divine love toward us, though afterwards he shows it more clearly from the contrary effect. However, it is an invaluable benefit that we can dare boldly to stand before God. By nature, indeed, we dread the presence of God, and quite rightly so; for since he is the Judge of the world, and our sins make us guilty, death and hell must come to our minds whenever we think of God. Hence comes the dread that I have mentioned, which makes people shun God as much as they can. But John says that the faithful are not afraid when people mention the last judgment, but on the contrary they go to God's tribunal confidently and cheerfully because they feel assured of his fatherly love. Our proficiency in faith can be measured by how well we are prepared in our minds to look forward to the day of judgment.

Like him. By these words the apostle means that we in our turn are required to resemble the image of God. So then, what God is in heaven, we are told to be in this world, so that we may be regarded as his children; for the image of God, when it appears in us, is the seal of his adoption, so to speak.

John, then, seems to place our confidence partly in works. It is as though he were denying that we can have a sure confidence as to salvation by relying on God's grace alone, without the help of works. But we are deceived if we believe this, because that would be to forget that the apostle is not here referring to the cause of salvation, but to what is added to it. And we readily agree that no one is reconciled to God through Christ without also being renewed in God's image; the one cannot be divorced from the other. The apostle rightly excludes from the confidence of grace all those in whom no image of God is seen, for it is certain that such people are wholly alien to the Spirit of God and to Christ.

Nor do we deny that newness of life, which is the effect of divine adoption, also serves to confirm confidence as a sort of secondary prop; but our foundation should be grace only. Indeed, John's doctrine would not otherwise seem consistent, for experience proves that our works always give cause for trembling. Therefore, we cannot come to God's tribunal with a tranquil heart unless we believe we are freely loved. If we are to go forward cheerfully and joyfully to meet Christ, we must have our faith fixed on his grace alone.

18. There is no fear in love. John now commends the excellency of this blessing by stating the contrary effect, for he says that we are continually tormented until God delivers us from misery and anguish by the remedy of his own love toward us. The meaning is that just as there is nothing more miserable than to be harassed by continual unrest, the knowledge of God's love toward us brings us the benefit of a peaceful calmness that is beyond the reach of fear. Hence we see what a singular gift of God it is to be favored with his love. Moreover, from this doctrine John presently draws an exhortation; but before he exhorts us to duty, he commends to us this gift of God, which by faith removes our fear.

This passage, I know, is explained differently by many interpreters. Some say that there is no fear in love because when we love God voluntarily, we are not constrained by force and fear to serve him. So according to them, servile fear is here set against voluntary reverence; and hence has arisen the distinction between servile fear and filial fear. Certainly I agree that when we willingly love God as a Father, we are no longer constrained by the fear of punishment; but this doctrine has nothing in common with this passage, for the apostle is only teaching us that when the love of God is seen by us and is known by faith, peace is given to our consciences, so that they no longer tremble and fear.

However, you may ask *when* perfect love expels fear; for since we are endued only with a taste of divine love toward us, we can never be wholly freed from fear. To this I answer that although fear is not wholly shaken off, it is really expelled when we flee to God as to a quiet haven where we are safe and free from all danger of shipwreck and storms, for our fear gives way to faith. So then, fear may not be so far expelled that we are no longer assailed by it, but it is expelled sufficiently for it not to torment us or impede the peace that we obtain by faith.

Fear has to do with punishment. Here the apostle amplifies still further the greatness of the grace he is talking about; for as it is a most miserable condition to suffer continual torments, we want nothing more than to present ourselves before God with a quiet conscience and a calm mind. Some people say that servants fear because they are thinking about punishment and that they do not perform their duty unless forced to do so, but this has nothing to do with what the apostle says here. So regarding the next clause, it does not match the context to say that anyone who fears is not perfect in love because he is not submitting to God willingly but would rather free himself from his service. On the contrary, the apostle reminds us that it is owing to unbelief when anyone fears—that is, has an uneasy mind—for the love of God, truly known, makes the heart tranquil.

19-21. We love because he first loved us. If anyone says, "I love God," yet hates his brother, he is a liar. For anyone who does not love his brother, whom he has seen, cannot love God, whom he has not seen. And he has given us this command: Whoever loves God must also love his brother.

19. We love. The Greek verb here may be either in the indicative or the imperative mood; but the former is the more suitable, because the apostle, I think, is repeating the preceding sentence, saying that as God has anticipated us by his free love, we ought in return to love him. For the apostle immediately infers that God ought to be loved in our brother, or that the love we have for God ought to be manifested toward our brother. However, if you prefer the imperative mood, the meaning would be nearly the same, that as God has freely loved us, we also ought to love him.

But this love cannot exist unless it generates brotherly love. Hence John says that people are liars if they boast that they love God while they hate their brothers.

But the reason the apostle gives does not seem valid enough, for it is a comparison between the less and the greater: if, he says, we do not love our brothers whom we see, much less can we love God who is invisible. Now there are obviously two exceptions, for the love that God has to us is from faith and does not flow from sight, as we find in 1 Peter 1:8; and second, the love of God is quite different from the love of human beings, for while God leads his people to love him through his infinite goodness, human beings are worthy of hatred. To this I answer that the apostle here takes for granted what ought no doubt to appear evident to us, that God offers himself to us in those people who bear his image, and that he requires the duties that he does not want himself to be performed to them. Surely the sharing of the same nature, the need of so many things, and mutual fellowship must attract us to mutual love, unless we are harder than iron. But John meant something else; he meant to show us how fallacious is the boast of every person who says that he loves God and yet does not love God's image that is before his eyes.

21. And he has given us this command. This is a stronger argument, drawn from the authority and doctrine of Christ; for the Master not only gave a command respecting the love of God, but also told us to love our brothers. We must therefore begin with God, so that there may also be a transition to human beings.

Chapter 5

1-5. Everyone who believes that Jesus is the Christ is born of God, and everyone who loves the father loves his child as well. This is how we know that we love the children of God: by loving God and carrying out his commands. This is love for God: to obey his commands. And his commands are not burdensome, for everyone born of God overcomes the world. This is the victory that has overcome the world, even our faith. Who is it that overcomes the world? Only he who believes that Jesus is the Son of God.

1. Everyone who believes. John gives another confirmation that faith and brotherly love are united; for since God regenerates us by faith, he must necessarily be loved by us as a Father; and this love embraces all his children. Faith, then, cannot be separated from love.

That Jesus is the Christ. The first truth is that **everyone who . . . is born of God . . . believes that Jesus is the Christ.** Here again we see that Christ alone is set up as the object of faith, as in him we find righteousness, life, and every blessing that can be desired and God in all that he is. Hence the only true way of believing is when we direct our minds to Jesus. Besides, to believe that he is the Christ is to hope to receive from him everything that has been promised concerning the Messiah.

Christ. This title is not given here without reason, for it designates the office to which our Saviour was appointed by the Father. Under the law, the full restoration of all things, including righteousness and happiness, was promised through the Messiah; today the whole of this is more clearly set out in the Gospel. So then, Jesus cannot be received as Christ if salvation is not sought from him, since this is why he was sent by the Father and is offered to us every day.

Hence the apostle says that all those who really believe have been **born of God,** for faith is far above the reach of the human mind, so that we must be drawn to Christ by our heavenly Father; none of us can ascend to him by our own strength. This is also what the apostle teaches us in his Gospel when he says that those who believe in the name of the one and only Son were "born not of natural descent" (John 1:13). And Paul says that "we have not received the spirit of the world, but the Spirit who is from God, that we may understand what God has freely given us" (1 Corinthians 2:12), for "no eye has seen, no ear has heard, no mind has conceived what God has prepared for those who love him" (1 Corinthians 2:9); the Spirit alone penetrates this mystery. Furthermore, as Christ is given to us for our sanctification and brings with him the Spirit of regeneration—in short, as he united us to his own body—this is another reason why no one can have faith unless he is born of God.

Everyone who loves the father loves his child as well. Augustine and some of the other ancient writers applied this to Christ, but not correctly. For although the apostle uses the singular number, he includes all the faithful; and the context plainly shows that his purpose was simply to trace brotherly love back to its source in faith. Indeed, this is an argument from the common course of nature; but what is seen among human beings is transferred to God.

Notice that the apostle does not speak in this way only of the faithful and ignore those who are outside, as though it is only the faithful who are to be loved, and no care and no account is to be made for unbelievers. John teaches us to begin with the godly but to go on to loving everyone without exception.

2. This is how we know. In these words John shows briefly what true love is—namely, that which exalts God. He has hitherto taught us that there is no true love unless our brothers are also loved, for this is always its effect. But now he teaches us that people are rightly and duly loved when God holds the primacy. And this is a necessary definition, for it often happens that we love people apart from God, as unholy and carnal friendships are only based on private advantage or some other evanescent goals. So, having first referred to the effect, John now refers to the cause; for his purpose is to show that mutual love should be cultivated in such a way that God may be honored.

To the love of God he adds keeping the law, and rightly so; for when we love God as our Father and Lord, reverence must necessarily be connected with love. Besides, God cannot be separated from himself. Since, then, he is the source of all righteousness and justice, anyone who loves him must necessarily have their heart prepared to obey the commands of righteousness. The love of God, then, is not idle or inactive.

But from this passage we also learn what keeping the law means. If we are only constrained by fear when we obey God by keeping his commands, we are very far from true obedience. The first principle is that our hearts should be devoted to God in willing reverence, and then that our life should be formed according to the rule of the law. This is what Moses meant when, in giving a summary of the law, he said, "O Israel, what does the LORD your God ask of you but . . . to love him . . . and to observe the LORD's commands and decrees?" (Deuteronomy 10:12-13).

3. His commands are not burdensome. This was added lest difficulties, as is usually the case, should damp or lessen our zeal, for those who pursue a godly and holy life with a cheerful mind and great ardor afterward grow weary, finding their strength inadequate. Therefore John, to rouse our efforts, says that God's **commands are not burdensome.**

But it may, on the other hand, be objected that we have found it quite otherwise by experience, and that Scripture testifies that the yoke of the law is insupportable. The reason is clear, for denying self is, as it were, a prelude to the keeping of the law, and how can we say that it is easy to deny ourselves? Indeed, since "the law is spiritual" (as Paul teaches in Romans 7:14), and we are nothing but flesh, there must be a great discord between us and the law of God. My answer to this is that this difficulty does not arise from the nature of the law, but from our corrupt flesh; and this is what Paul explicitly says. After saying that it was impossible for the law to confer righteousness on us, he immediately puts the blame on our flesh.

This explanation fully reconciles what is said by Paul and by David, who appear to be wholly contradictory. Paul makes the law the minister of death, saying that it does nothing but bring on us God's wrath, that it was given to increase sin, that it lives in order to kill us. David, on the other hand, says that it is "sweeter than honey" and "more precious than gold"

(Psalm 19:10); and among other recommendations he mentions the follow-ing: it revives the soul (Psalm 19:7), gives joy to the heart (Psalm 19:8), and preserves life (Psalm 119:50). But Paul compares the law with corrupt human nature; hence arises the conflict. David shows how people think and feel when God has renewed them by his Spirit; hence the sweetness and delight of which the flesh knows nothing. And John has not omitted this difference, for his words **his commands are not burdensome** are confined to God's children and should not be taken generally. He means that through the power of the Spirit the law is not burdensome and thus it is not wearisome to us to obey God.

However, the question does not yet seem to be fully answered, for the faithful, though ruled by God's Spirit, still have a hard struggle with their own flesh; and however much they may labor, they still hardly perform half of their duty. Indeed, they almost fail under their burden. We see that Paul groaned like a captive and exclaimed that he was wretched because he could not serve God fully. My reply to this is that the law is said to be easy insofar as we are endued with heavenly power and overcome the lusts of the flesh. For however the flesh may resist, the faithful find that there is no real enjoyment except in following God.

Notice also that John does not just speak about the law, which con-tains nothing but commands, but links with it God's fatherly indulgence, by which the rigor of the law is mitigated. Knowing that we are gra-ciously forgiven by the Lord when our works do not fully conform to the law makes us far more prompt to obey, as we find in Psalm 130:4—"with you there is forgiveness; therefore you are feared." That is why keeping the law is easy—because the faithful, being sustained by forgiveness, are not despondent when they come short of what they ought to be. The apostle reminds us, too, that we must fight ("overcome") in order to serve the Lord, for the whole world hinders us from going where the Lord calls us. So then, it is only the person who courageously resists the world who keeps the law.

4. This is the victory. John had said that **everyone born of God has overcome the world.** Now he sets out the way of overcoming it, for it might still be asked where this victory comes from. John makes the victory over the world dependent on **faith.**

This passage is remarkable, for though Satan continually repeats his dreadful and horrible onsets, the Spirit of God declares that we are beyond the reach of danger; he removes our fear and animates us to fight with courage. And the past is more emphatic than the present or the future, for John says, **This is the victory that has overcome,** so that we might feel certain, as though the enemy had already been put to flight. Indeed, it is true that our warfare continues throughout life, that we are in conflicts every day, and that various new battles are stirred up against us on every side at every moment by the enemy; but God does not arm us just for one day, and faith is not that of just one day, but is the perpetual work of the Holy Spirit. We already share in victory, as though we had already conquered.

This confidence does not, however, make us indifferent but makes us always anxiously intent on fighting. For the Lord tells people to be certain, though he does not want them to be complacent; on the contrary, he says that they have already overcome in order that they may fight more courageously and more strenuously.

The world. This has a wide meaning here, for it includes whatever is against God's Spirit; thus, the corruption of our nature is a part of the world—all lusts, all Satan's crafts—in short, whatever leads us away from God. Having such a force to contend with, we have an immense war to carry on, and we would already have been conquered before coming to the contest, and would be conquered a hundred times a day, if God had not promised us the victory. But by promising us the victory God encourages us to fight. This promise secures for us God's invincible power for all time, and it annihilates all human strength. The apostle does not teach us here that God only brings *some* help to us, so that with his aid we may be able to resist; he makes victory dependent on faith alone, and faith receives from elsewhere what enables it to overcome. People who sing triumph to their own power take away from God what is his own.

5. Who is it that overcomes the world? This is a reason for the previous sentence; that is, we conquer by faith because we derive strength from Christ. Paul too says, "I can do everything through him who gives me strength" (Philippians 4:13). So then, if we are to conquer Satan and the world and not succumb to our flesh, we must be unsure about ourselves and rely only on Christ's power.

Only he who believes. John means a real apprehension of Christ or an effectual laying hold on him, by which we apply his power to ourselves.

6-9. This is the one who came by water and blood—Jesus Christ. He

did not come by water only, but by water and blood. And it is the Spirit who testifies, because the Spirit is the truth. For there are three that testify in heaven: the Father, the Word and the Holy Spirit, and these three are one. And there are three that testify on earth: the Spirit, the water and the blood; and the three are in agreement. We accept man's testimony, but God's testimony is greater because it is the testimony of God, which he has given about his Son. (See NIV margin.)

6. This is the one who came. In order that our faith may rest safely on Christ, John says that the real substance of the shadows of the law appears in Christ.

By water and blood. I have no doubt this alludes to the ancient rites of the law. Moreover, the comparison is intended not only to teach us that the law of Moses was abolished by the coming of Christ, but so we will seek in him the fulfillment of those things that the ceremonies formerly typified. Though they were of various kinds, the apostle uses these two terms to denote the whole of holiness and righteousness. **Water** washed all filth away, so that people might come before God pure and clean; and **blood** made expiation and pledged a full reconciliation with God. The law only foreshadowed by external symbols what was to be really and fully achieved by the Messiah.

So John proves that Jesus is the Christ who had previously been promised, because he brought with him that by which he sanctifies us wholly.

There is no doubt about the **blood** by which Christ reconciled God, but there may be some question about how he came **by water**. It is unlikely that the reference is to baptism. I am sure John here is referring to the fruit and effect of what he recorded in the Gospel story, for what he says there—that water and blood flowed from the side of Christ—is no doubt to be seen as a miracle. I know that such a thing does naturally happen to the dead, but it happened because God planned that Christ's side should become the fountain of blood and water so that the faithful would know that cleansing (of which the ancient baptisms were types) is found in him, and so they might know that what all the sprinklings of blood had indicated was now fulfilled.

And it is the Spirit who testifies. John shows in this clause how the faithful know and feel the power of Christ; it is because the Spirit makes believers certain. And, so their faith might not vacillate, he adds that a full and real firmness or stability is produced by the testimony of the Spirit. He calls the Spirit **the truth** because his authority cannot be doubted and should be quite enough for us.

7-8. There are three that testify. The whole of this verse has been omitted by some people. Jerome thinks that this has happened through design rather than through mistake. But as even the Greek editions do not agree, I dare not assert anything on the subject. However, since the passage flows better when this clause is added, and as I see that it is found in the best manuscripts, I am inclined to accept it as the true reading. The meaning would be that God, in order to confirm our faith in Christ most abundantly, testifies in three ways that we ought to rest in him. Just as our faith acknowledges three persons in the one divine essence, so that faith is called in three ways to Christ, that it may rest on him.

And these three are one. John is not referring to essence but to consent; this is like saying that the Father and his eternal Word and Spirit harmoniously testify the same thing about Christ. There is no doubt that the Father, the Word, and the Spirit are said to be one in the same sense in which afterwards the blood and the water and the Spirit are said to be **in agreement.**

As the Spirit, who is one witness, is mentioned twice, it seems to be an unnecessary repetition. To this I reply that since the Spirit testifies of Christ in various ways, it is right to ascribe a double testimony to him. As the Father, together with his eternal wisdom and Spirit, declares Jesus to be the Christ authoritatively, so to speak, so in this case the sole majesty of the Deity is to be considered by us. As the Spirit, dwelling in our hearts, is a deposit, a pledge, and a seal, to confirm that decree, so he speaks again on earth by his grace.

But since not all scholars accept this reading, I will expound what follows as though the apostle was referring only to the witnesses on the earth.

There are three. John applies what he had said about **the water and the blood** to his own purpose, in order that those who reject Christ might have no excuse; for he proves with very strong and clear testimonies that Christ is he who had previously been promised. Water and blood, being the pledges and effects of salvation, truly testify that he had been sent by God. John adds a third witness, **the Spirit.** The Holy Spirit has first place, for without him the water and blood would have flowed without any benefit; it is he who seals on our hearts the testimony of the water and blood; it is he who by his power makes the fruit of Christ's death come to us. Indeed, he makes the blood shed for our redemption penetrate into our hearts, or, to put it in a nutshell, he makes Christ with all his blessings become ours. So also Paul, when he says that Christ by his resurrection was declared to be the Son of God, also says this was "through the Spirit" (Romans 1:4). Whatever signs of divine glory may shine in Christ, they would be obscure to us and escape our vision if the Holy Spirit did not open the eyes of faith for us.

Readers may now understand why John adduced **the Spirit** as a witness together with **the water and the blood**. It was because it is the Spirit's unique function to cleanse our consciences by the blood of Christ, to cause the cleansing which that blood brought to be effective. On this subject some remarks are made at the beginning of 1 Peter, where that apostle uses nearly the same way of speaking, saying that the Holy Spirit cleanses our hearts by the sprinkling of the blood of Christ.

From these words we may learn that faith does not lay hold on a bare or empty Christ, but that his power is life-giving. Why has Christ been sent to the earth but to reconcile God by the sacrifice of his death and to perform the office of washing, allotted to him by the Father?

However, it may be objected that the distinction here mentioned is superfluous, because Christ cleansed us by expiating our sins by his death, and so the apostle mentions the same thing twice. Certainly I agree that cleansing is included in expiation; that is why I made no distinction between the water and the blood. But if we consider our own weakness, we shall readily acknowledge that it is not in vain or without reason that blood is distinguished from the water. Besides, the apostle is alluding, as we have said, to the rites of the law; and God, on account of human weakness, had previously appointed not only sacrifices but also washings. The apostle wanted to show distinctly that the reality of both has been seen in Christ, and on this account he had already said that **he did not come by water only** (verse 6). He means that this is not only part of our salvation that is found in Christ, but the whole of it; nothing is to be sought elsewhere.

9a. We accept man's testimony.

Reasoning from the less to the greater, John proves how ungrateful we are when we reject Christ, who has been approved by God; for if in worldly affairs we stand against people's words when they lie and deceive, how unreasonable it is that God should have less credit given to him when sitting on his own throne, where he is the supreme judge. So then, our own corruption alone prevents us from receiving Christ, since he gives us every proof of his power. Besides, it is not only what the Spirit imprints on our hearts that John calls the testimony of God, but also what we derive from the water and the blood. For that power of cleansing and expiating was not earthly but heavenly. Hence the blood of Christ is not to be estimated according to the common human manner, but we must rather look to the intention of God, who ordained it for blotting out our sins, and also to the divine efficacy that comes from it.

9b-12. But God's testimony is greater because it is the testimony of God, which he has given about his Son. Anyone who believes in the Son of God has this testimony in his heart. Anyone who does not believe God has made him out to be a liar, because he has not believed the testimony God has given about his Son. And this is the testimony: God has given us eternal life, and this life is in his Son. He who has the Son has life; he who does not have the Son of God does not have life.

9b. But God's testimony is greater. Having reminded us that God deserves to be believed much more than human beings, the apostle now adds that we can have no faith in God without believing in Christ, because God sets him alone before us and makes us stand in him. Hence he infers that we believe in Christ safely and with tranquil minds, because God by his authority warrants our faith. He does not say that God speaks outwardly, but that every one of the godly feels within that God is the author of his faith. Hence it appears how different faith is from a fading opinion dependent on something else.

10. Anyone who does not believe. As the faithful possess the benefit of knowing themselves to be beyond the danger of erring, because they have God as their foundation, so John makes the ungodly to be guilty of extreme blasphemy because they charge God with falsehood. Doubtless nothing is more valued by God than his own truth; therefore, no wrong more atrocious can be done to him than to rob him of this honor. So then, in order to induce us to believe, John takes an argument from the opposite side; for if making God out to be a liar is a horrible and execrable impiety, because it denies him what especially belongs to him, who would not dread to withhold faith from the Gospel, in which God wants himself to be counted singularly true and faithful? This ought to be carefully noticed.

Some people wonder why God commends faith so much, and why

unbelief is so severely condemned. But the glory of God is implicated in this, for since he planned to show a special example of his truth in the Gospel, all who reject Christ as offered to them in the Gospel are leaving nothing to him. Therefore, though people may in other parts of their lives be like angels, their sanctity is diabolical as long as they reject Christ. The beginning of true religion is obediently to embrace this doctrine that he has so strongly confirmed by his testimony.

11. God has given us eternal life. Having now shown the benefit, John invites us to believe. It is, indeed, a reverence due to God when we immediately receive, as being beyond controversy, whatever he declares to us. But since he freely offers life to us, our ingratitude will be intolerable unless we receive with prompt faith this sweet and lovely doctrine. Doubtless the apostle's words are intended to show that we should not only reverently obey the Gospel, lest we affront God, but also that we should love it because it brings us eternal life. From this we also learn what is especially to be sought in the Gospel—namely, the free gift of salvation. In the Gospel, God exhorts us to repentance and fear, and this should not be separated from the grace of Christ.

But the apostle, in order to keep us altogether in Christ, repeats that life is found in him. This is like saying that no other way of obtaining life has been appointed for us by God the Father. The apostle briefly includes here three things. First, we are all given up to death until God in his unmerited favor restores us to life; for John clearly says that life is a gift from God, and hence it follows that we are destitute of it, and it cannot be acquired by merit. Second, he teaches us that this life is conferred on us by the Gospel, because there the goodness and fatherly love of God is made known to us. Lastly, he says that we cannot share in this life without believing in Christ.

12. He who does not have the Son of God. This confirms the last sentence. It should, indeed, have been enough that God made life to be in none but Christ, so that it might be sought in him; but lest anyone should turn away to someone else, John excludes from the hope of life all who do not seek it in Christ. We know what it is to have Christ, for he is possessed only by faith. So John shows that all who are separated from the body of Christ are without life.

But this seems inconsistent with reason; for history shows that there have been great men, endued with heroic virtues, who were wholly unacquainted with Christ, and it seems unreasonable for people of such eminence not to be honored. To this I answer that we are greatly mistaken if we think that whatever is eminent in our eyes is approved by God; for as it says in Luke 16:15, "What is highly valued among men is detestable in God's sight." As the condition of our heart is hidden from us, we are satisfied with external appearances; but God sees that underneath is concealed the foulest filth. Therefore, it is no wonder if specious virtues, flowing from an impure heart and leading to no right end, smell bad to him. Besides, where does purity come from, and a genuine regard for religion, if it is not from the Spirit of Christ? There is, then, nothing worthy of praise except in Christ.

Furthermore, there is another consideration that removes every doubt. Human righteousness does not produce the remission of sins. If you take such righteousness away, the sure curse of God and eternal death awaits. It is Christ alone who reconciles the Father to us, as he has once for all pacified God by the sacrifice of the cross. Hence it follows that God is propitious to no one who is not in Christ, nor is there righteousness other than in him.

If anyone objects that Cornelius was accepted by God before he was called to the faith of the Gospel (Acts 10:2), I answer briefly that God sometimes deals with us in such a way that the seed of faith appears immediately on the first day. Cornelius had no clear and distinct knowledge of Christ, but as he had some perception of God's mercy, he must at the same time have understood something of a Mediator. But as God acts in secret and wonderful ways, let us disregard such unprofitable speculations and hold only to the plain way of salvation that he has made known to us.

13-15. I write these things to you who believe in the name of the Son of God so that you may know that you have eternal life. This is the assurance we have in approaching God: that if we ask anything according to his will, he hears us. And if we know that he hears us—whatever we ask—we know that we have what we asked of him.

13. I write these things to you. There should be daily progress in faith, and so the apostle says that he was writing to those **who believe in the name of the Son of God,** so that they might believe more firmly and with greater certainty and thus enjoy a fuller confidence as to eternal life. So then, the use of doctrine is not only to initiate the ignorant in the knowledge of Christ, but also to confirm more and more those who have already been taught. Therefore, it becomes us to attend assiduously to the duty of learning, so that our faith may increase throughout our life. For there are still in us many remnants of unbelief, and our faith is so weak that what we believe is not yet really believed unless there is fuller confirmation.

But we should notice the way in which faith is confirmed. It is by having the office and power of Christ explained to us. The apostle says that he wrote these things (that is, that eternal life is to be sought only in Christ) in order that those who were already believers might believe—that is, make progress in believing. It is therefore the duty of a godly teacher, in order to confirm disciples in the faith, to extol the grace of Christ as much as possible, so that we may be satisfied with that and seek nothing else.

The apostle also teaches us in this passage that Christ is the unique object of faith and that the hope of salvation is added to the faith that we have in his name. In this case the point of believing is that we become God's children and heirs.

14. This is the assurance. John commends the faith that he mentioned by its fruit; or he shows where our confidence especially resides; namely, godly people dare to confidently call on God. Paul, too, says in Ephesians 3:12 that by faith we have access to God with confidence; and in Romans 8:15 he says that the Spirit enables us to cry "*Abba*, Father." If we were driven away from access to God, there is no doubt that nothing could make us more miserable. On the other hand, provided this asylum is open to us, we can be happy even in extreme evil. This one thing makes our troubles blessed, because we surely know that God will be our deliverer; and relying on his fatherly love toward us, we flee to him.

Let us, then, bear in mind the apostle's declaration that calling on God is the chief test of our faith, and that we do not call on God truly or in faith unless we are sure that our prayers will not be in vain. The apostle denies that we are endued with faith if we are doubtful and hesitate.

According to his will. By this expression John wanted to remind us incidentally about the right way of praying, which is when people subject their own wishes to God. Although God has promised to do whatever his people may ask, he does not allow them an unbridled liberty to ask whatever may come into their heads. He has also prescribed for them a law according to which they are to pray. And doubtless nothing is better for us than this restriction; for if each of us was allowed to ask whatever we pleased, and if God were to indulge us in our wishes, it would go very badly for us. We do not know what is expedient for us; we boil over with corrupt and harmful desires. But God supplies a double remedy, lest we should pray other than according to his own will.

He teaches us by his Word what he wants us to ask, and he has also set his Spirit over us as our guide and ruler, to restrain our feelings so as not to allow them to wander beyond due bounds. We do not know what or how to pray, says Paul, but the Spirit helps us in our weakness and excites in us groans that words cannot express (Romans 8:26). We should ask the Lord to direct and guide our prayers, for, as I said, God in his promises has fixed the right way of praying.

15. And if we know. This is not a superfluous repetition, as it seems to be. What the apostle said generally about the success of prayer is now confirmed in a special manner: godly people pray to God only for what they obtain. But when he says that all the prayers of the faithful are heard, he is speaking about right and humble petitions and such as are consistent with the rule of obedience. The faithful do not give free rein to their desires or indulge in anything that pleases them, but always in their prayers consider what God commands.

This, then, is an application of the general doctrine to everyone's special and private benefit, lest the faithful should doubt that God is propitious to the prayers of each individual, so that with quiet minds they may wait until the Lord does what they pray for. So then, being relieved of all trouble and anxiety, they may cast on God the burden of their cares. This ease and security should not, however, reduce the earnestness of their prayer, for whoever is certain of a happy event should not stop praying to God. The certainty of faith by no means generates indifference or sloth. The apostle meant that all those in need should be calm when they have deposited their sighs with God.

16-18. If anyone sees his brother commit a sin that does not lead to death, he should pray and God will give him life. I refer to those whose sin does not lead to death. There is a sin that leads to death. I am not saying that he should pray about that. All wrongdoing is sin, and there is sin that does not lead to death. We know that anyone born of God does not continue to sin; the one who was born of God keeps him safe, and the evil one does not touch him.

16. If anyone. The apostle extends the benefits of faith still further, so that our prayers may also help our brothers. It is a wonderful thing that as soon as we are oppressed, God kindly invites us to himself and is ready to give us help; but his hearing us ask for others is no small confirmation to our faith, in order that we may be fully assured that we will never meet with a rebuff in our own case.

The apostle also exhorts us to care for each other's salvation; and he would also have us regard our brothers' falls as stimuli to prayer. Surely it is an iron hardness to be touched with no pity when we see souls redeemed by Christ's blood going to ruin. But he shows that there is a remedy at hand by which brother can help brother. Anyone who will pray for the perishing will, he says, restore him to life. God will grant the life of a brother in answer to your prayers. Such a great benefit should stimulate us to ask forgiveness of sins for our brothers. And when the apostle recommends sympathy to us, he also reminds us how much we ought to avoid the cruelty of condemning our brothers or an extreme severity in despairing of their salvation.

A sin that does not lead to death. In order that we do not give up all hope of the salvation of those who sin, John shows that God does not punish their falls so grievously as to repudiate them. Hence it follows that we should regard them as brothers, since God retains them in the number of his children. John denies that such sins **lead to death**—not only those by which the saints offend every day, but even when it happens that God's wrath is grievously provoked by them. For as long as there is room for pardon, death does not entirely retain its dominion.

However, the apostle does not here distinguish between venial and mortal sin, as was often done afterwards. That distinction is altogether foolish. Some theologians acknowledge that there is hardly a sin that leads to death, unless there is the grossest, almost tangible baseness. Thus they think that the greatest filth may be mere venial sins if they are hidden in the soul. In short, they suppose that all the fruits of original sin, as long as they do not appear outwardly, are washed away with a little sprinkling of holy water! And what wonder is this, since they do not regard as blasphemous sins any doubts about God's grace or any lusts or evil desires unless they are consented to? If the human soul is assailed by unbelief, if impatience tempts us to rage against God, whatever monstrous lusts may entice us, all these are too trivial to be counted as sins, they say, at least after baptism. It is no wonder, then, that they make the greatest of crimes into venial offenses, for they weigh them in their own scales and not in God's.

But the faithful should count it as undoubted truth that whatever is contrary to God's law is sin and in its nature leads to death. Wherever the law is transgressed, there is sin and death.

What does the apostle mean then? He denies that sins lead to death if they are not punished by God even though the transgressors deserve death. Therefore, he is not judging sins in themselves but according to God's fatherly kindness, which pardons the guilty even where there is fault. In short, God does not give over to death those whom he has restored to life, though it is not by their doing that they are not alienated from life.

There is a sin that leads to death. I have already said that this refers to the sin to which no hope of forgiveness is left. But what is this? It must be very atrocious, since God punishes it as severely as this. It may be gathered from the context that it is not, as people say, a partial fall or a transgression of a single commandment but rather apostasy, by which people wholly alienate themselves from God. For the apostle later adds that the children of God do not **continue to sin**; that is, they do not forsake God and wholly surrender themselves to Satan to be his slaves. No wonder such a defection leads to death, for God never deprives his own people of the grace of the Spirit, but they always have some spark of true religion. So then, people who fall away like this and have no fear of God must be reprobate and given up to destruction.

If anyone asks whether the door of salvation is closed against their repentance, the answer is obvious, for since they are given up to a reprobate mind and are destitute of the Holy Spirit, they cannot do anything other than obstinately become worse and worse and add more and more sins. Moreover, as the sin and blasphemy against the Spirit always brings with it a defection of this kind, there is no doubt that it is pointed out here.

But again, you may ask what evidence tells us that someone's fall is fatal. If we could not be certain of this, the apostle would not have been able to say that they were not to pray for a sin of this kind. It is right, then, to decide sometimes whether there is still hope. With this, indeed, I agree, and it is evident beyond dispute from this passage; but as this very seldom happens, and as God sets before us the infinite riches of his grace and bids us be merciful according to his own example, we should not rashly conclude that anyone has brought the judgment of eternal death on himself. On the contrary, love should make us hope for good. But if some people's impiety does not appear to us anything other than hopeless, as though the Lord pointed it out by his finger, we should not argue with God's just judgment or seek to be more merciful than he is.

17. All wrongdoing is sin, and there is sin that does not lead to death. This passage may be explained in various ways. If you take it as a contrast, the sense would fit: "Though all wrongdoing is sin, every sin does not lead to death." Equally suitable is another meaning: "As sin can be attributed to every wrongdoing, it follows that every sin does not lead to death." Some people take **all wrongdoing** to mean complete unrighteousness, as though the apostle were saying that the sin of which he spoke was the summit of unrighteousness. However, I am more disposed to adopt the first or second explanation; and as the result is nearly the same, I leave it to the judgment of readers to decide which of the two is the more appropriate.

18. We know that anyone born of God. If you suppose that God's children are wholly pure and free from all sin, as the fanatics argue, then the apostle is inconsistent, for he would be taking away the duty brothers have to pray for one another. So then, he says that those who do **not continue to sin** are not wholly falling away from God's grace; and hence he infers that prayer should be made for all God's children because they do not sin to death. A proof is added—namely, that **the one who was born of God keeps him safe** and does not allow himself to be so led astray as to lose all sense of religion and to surrender himself wholly to the devil and the flesh.

The evil one does not touch him. This refers to a deadly wound. God's children do not remain untouched by Satan's assaults, but they ward off his blows with the shield of faith, so that they do not penetrate the heart. Hence spiritual life is never extinguished in believers. Though the faithful do fall through the weakness of the flesh, they groan under the burden of sin, loathe themselves, and do not cease to fear God.

Keeps him safe. If we were the keepers of our own salvation, it would be a miserable protection. Therefore, Christ asks the Father to keep us, saying that it is not done by our own strength. The faithful do not themselves have the power to keep themselves safe, but they should resist Satan so they may never be fatally wounded by his arrows. And we know that we fight with no other weapons but those of God.

19-21. We know that we are children of God, and that the whole world is under the control of the evil one. We know also that the Son of God has come and has given us understanding, so that we may know him who is true. And we are in him who is true—even in his Son Jesus

Christ. He is the true God and eternal life. Dear children, keep yourselves from idols.

19. We know that we are children of God. John deduces an exhortation
from his previous doctrine; what he had declared to be common to God's
children, he now applies to those to whom he was writing. He did this to
stimulate them to beware of sin and to encourage them to repel Satan's
attacks.

Notice that it is only true faith that applies the grace of God to us, for
the apostle acknowledges as faithful only those who have the dignity of
being God's children. He does not put probable conjecture for confidence,
for he says that we **know**. The meaning is that as we have been born of
God, we should strive to prove by our separation from the world and by
the sanctity of our life that it is not in vain that we have been called to so
great an honor.

This warning is very necessary for all godly people, for wherever they
look, Satan has his lures prepared, by which he seeks to draw them away
from God. It would be difficult, then, for them to keep their course if they
did not value their calling so highly that they disregard all the hindrances of
the world. So then, in order to be well-prepared for the contest, these two
things must be borne in mind: the world is wicked, and our calling is from
God.

The whole world is under the control of the evil one. No doubt the
apostle includes the whole human race here. There is no reason why we
should hesitate to shun the world, which holds God in contempt and gives
itself up to the bondage of Satan; nor is there any reason why we should
fear its enmity, because it is alienated from God. In short, since corruption
pervades all nature, the faithful ought to devote themselves to self-denial;
and since nothing but wickedness and corruption is seen in the world, they
will have to disregard flesh and blood so they may follow God. We should
also add that since God is the one who has called them, it is under his protection that they may oppose all the machinations of the world and Satan.

20. We know also that the Son of God has come. As the children of
God are attacked on every side, the apostle encourages and exhorts them to
persevere in resisting their enemies. This is because they fight under God's
banner and know for certain that they are ruled by his Spirit; but now John
reminds them where this knowledge is especially to be found.

And has given us understanding. God has been made known to us in such a way that there is now no need to doubt. It is not without reason that the apostle dwells on this point; for unless our faith is really founded on God, we will never stand firm in the battle. The apostle shows that we have obtained a sure knowledge of the true God through Christ, so that we will not fluctuate in uncertainty.

So that we may know him who is true. By this John does not mean one who tells the truth, but One who is really God; and he calls him this to distinguish him from all idols. He is **true** as opposed to fictitious. There is a similar passage in John 17:3: "This is eternal life: that they may know you, the only true God, and Jesus Christ, whom you have sent." The apostle rightly ascribes to Christ this function of illuminating our minds as to the knowledge of God. Since he is the only true image of the invisible God, the only interpreter of the Father, the only guide of life, and the life and light of the world and the truth, as soon as we leave him, we necessarily become vain in our own devices.

Christ is said to have **given us understanding** not only because he shows us in the Gospel what sort of being the true God is, and also illuminates us by his Spirit, but because in Christ himself we have God manifested in the flesh, as Paul says: "in Christ all the fullness of the Deity lives," and "in [him] are hidden all the treasures of wisdom and knowledge" (Colossians 2:9, 3). Thus it is that God's face in a way appears to us in Christ—not that there was no knowledge, or a doubtful knowledge, of God before the coming of Christ, but that now he reveals himself more fully and more clearly. This is what Paul says in 2 Corinthians 4:6: "God, who said, 'Let light shine out of darkness,' made his light shine in our hearts to give us the light of the knowledge of the glory of God in the face of Christ."

Notice too that this gift is peculiar to those who are chosen. Christ indeed kindles the torch of his Gospel for everyone indiscriminately; but we do not all have the eyes of our mind opened to see it. On the contrary, Satan spreads the veil of blindness over many people. The apostle, then, means the light that Christ kindles within the hearts of his people and that, once it is kindled, is never extinguished, though in some people it may for a time be smothered.

And we are in him who is true. By these words John reminds us how efficacious is the knowledge that he mentions. By it we are united to Christ and become one with God, for it has a living root, fixed in the heart, by which it comes about that God lives in us and we in him. When the apostle says that we are **in him who is true—even in his Son**, he seems to be expressing the manner of our union with God—namely, that we are in God through Christ.

He is the true God and eternal life. The Arians have attempted to escape this passage, but we have here a remarkable testimony to the divinity of Christ. The Arians apply this passage to the Father, as though the apostle were repeating that he is the true God. But nothing could be more cold than such a repetition. John has already said twice that the true God is he who has been made known to us in Christ. Why should he add again, **He is the true God**? This applies most appropriately to Christ, for after teaching us that Christ is the guide by whose hand we are led to God, John now, by way of amplification, affirms that Christ is that God, lest we should think we are to look elsewhere. He confirms this by what is added: **and eternal life**. It is doubtless the same thing to be **the true God and eternal life**. I say, then, that Christ is rightly called **eternal life**, and no one can deny that this manner of speaking occurs all the time in John.

The meaning is that when we have Christ, we enjoy the true and eternal God, for nowhere else is he to be sought, and, second, that we come to share in eternal life because it is offered to us in Christ, though it is hidden in the Father. The origin of life is indeed the Father, but the fountain from which we are to draw it is Christ.

21. Keep yourselves from idols. Although this is a separate sentence, it is a sort of appendix to the preceding doctrine. The life-giving light of the Gospel ought to scatter and dissipate not only darkness but also all mists from the minds of the godly. The apostle not only condemns idolatry but commands us to beware of all images and idols. In this way he intimates that the worship of God cannot continue uncorrupted and pure whenever people begin to be in love with idols or images, for superstition is so innate in us that the least occasion will infect us with its contagion. Dry wood when coals are put under it will not burn as easily as idolatry lays hold on and engrosses our minds when it is given the chance. And who does not see that images are sparks, or rather torches, that are sufficient to set the whole world on fire?

The apostle is not only speaking of statues, but also of altars and all that goes with superstitions. It is ridiculous to pervert this passage and say that it applies only to the statues of Jupiter and Mercury and so on, as though the apostle were not teaching generally that religion is corrupted whenever a physical form is ascribed to God, or wherever statues and pictures form part of his worship. Let us then remember that we should carefully continue in the spiritual worship of God, so as to banish far from us everything that may turn us aside to gross and carnal superstitions.

2 John
by Matthew Henry

2 John

Here we find a canonical letter written, principally, not only to a single person, but to someone of the softer sort (**the chosen lady**). And why not to one of that gender? Regarding the privilege and dignity of the Gospel and redemption, "there is neither . . . male nor female"; they are "one in Christ Jesus" (Galatians 3:28). Our Lord himself neglected his own meal in order to commune with the woman of Samaria, to show her the fountain of life; and when he was dying on the cross, he chose to leave his blessed mother to the care of the disciple whom he loved and thereby instructed him to respect female disciples in the future.

It was to one of the same gender that our Lord chose to appear first after his return from the grave, and by her to send the news of his resurrection to the apostles. Afterwards we find a zealous Priscilla acquitting herself so well in her Christian race, and particularly in hazardous service to the apostle Paul, that she is often mentioned before her husband. Both the apostle himself and all the Gentile churches were ready to acknowledge their gratitude to Priscilla as well as to her husband. No wonder, then, that a heroine in the Christian religion, honored by divine providence and distinguished by divine grace, should be dignified also by an apostle's letter.

The apostle greets an honorable lady and her children (1-3).
He recommends to them faith and love (4-6).
He warns them of deceivers and to take care of themselves (7-8).

He teaches how to treat those who do not bring the doctrine of Christ (9-11).
Leaving other things for personal conversation, he concludes the letter (12-13).

1-2. The elder, To the chosen lady and her children, whom I love in the truth—and not I only, but also all who know the truth—because of the truth, which lives in us and will be with us forever.

Ancient letters began, as here, with a greeting and good wishes; as far as possible, religion consecrates old forms and turns compliments into real expressions of life and love. Here we have, as usual:

1. The person who is sending the greeting—not expressed by name, but by a chosen description, **the elder**. The expression, style, and love indicate that the penman was the same as that of the previous letter; he is now **the elder**, emphatically and eminently so—possibly the oldest apostle now living; the chief **elder** in the church of God. **The elder** in the ancient house of Israel was revered or to be reverenced; much more he who is so in the Gospel—the Israel of God. An old disciple is honorable, and an old apostle and leader of disciples the more so. John was now old in holy service and experience, he had tasted much of heaven, and he was much nearer than when at first he believed.

2. The people who are being greeted—a noble Christian, a **chosen lady and her children**. A **lady**, a person eminent by birth, education, and estate. It is good that the Gospel reaches such people. It is a pity if lords and ladies are not acquainted with the Lord Christ and his religion; they owe more to him than others do, though usually "not many of noble birth" are called (see 1 Corinthians 1:26). Here is a pattern for high-ranking people of the same sex.

Chosen lady. Not only a choice one, but one chosen by God. It is lovely and beautiful to see ladies, by living in a holy way, demonstrate that God has chosen them.

And her children. Probably the lady was a widow; she **and her children** were then the principal part of the family, and so this may be styled an economical letter. Families may well be written to and encouraged and further directed in their domestic love, order, and duties. We see that children may well be taken notice of in Christian letters; we may help them by encouraging and warning them. Those who love and commend them will be apt to inquire after them.

This **lady and her children** were further distinguished by the respect paid to them:

(a) By the apostle himself—**whom I love in the truth** or "in truth"—that is, "whom I sincerely and heartily love." The disciple who was loved had learned the art or practice of love; and he especially loved those who loved the Lord who loved him.

(b) By all her Christian acquaintances, all the religious people who knew her—**and not I only, but also all who know the truth**. Virtue and goodness in high places shine brightly; truth demands to be acknowledged, and those who see evidences of pure religion should confess and attest them. It is a good sign and great duty to love and value religion in others.

Here is the ground of this love and respect paid to this **lady and her children—because of the truth** (or, because of true religion) **which lives in us and will be with us forever.** Christian love is founded upon the appearance of living, Christian religion. Likeness should give rise to affection; those who love truth and piety in themselves should love it in others too, or love others on account of it. The apostle and the other Christians loved this lady not so much for her high rank as for her holiness, not so much for her bounty as for her serious Christianity. We should not be religious merely by fits and starts, uncertain moods and moons; religion should continually dwell within us, in our minds and hearts, in our faith and love. It is to be hoped that where religion once truly lives, it will stay forever. The spirit of Christianity, we may suppose, will not be totally extinguished; it **will be with us forever.**

3-4. Grace, mercy and peace from God the Father and from Jesus Christ, the Father's Son, will be with us in truth and love. It has given me great joy to find some of your children walking in the truth, just as the Father commanded us.

Here we see, first, the greeting, which is indeed an apostolic benediction: **Grace, mercy and peace from God the Father and from Jesus Christ, the Father's Son, will be with us in truth and love.** Sacred love pours out blessings upon this honorable Christian family; to those who have, more will be given. Notice from whom these blessings are craved: (1) **from God the Father,** the God of grace; he is the fountain of blessedness and of all the blessings that must bring us to him. And (2) **from Jesus Christ;** he is the Author and Communicator of these heavenly blessings and is distinguished by this emphatic description, **the Father's Son.** No one else can be a Son like he is, "the radiance of God's glory and the exact representation of his being" (Hebrews 1:3), who, with the Father, is "eternal life" (1 John 1:2; 5:20).

From these divine persons the apostle craves (1) **Grace**—divine favor and goodwill, the spring of all good things; it is **grace**, indeed, that any spiritual blessing should be conferred on sinful mortals. (2) **Mercy**—free pardon and forgiveness; those who are already rich in **grace** need continual forgiveness. (3) **Peace**—tranquillity of spirit and serenity of conscience, in an assured reconciliation with God, together with all safe and sanctified outward prosperity. These are all desired **in truth and love**—by sincere and ardent affection in the person sending the greeting (in faith and love he prays for them—**from God the Father and from Jesus Christ**) or as productive of continued **truth and love** in the people he is greeting. These blessings will continually preserve true faith and love in **the chosen lady and her children**!

Second, we see how the apostle congratulates this excellent lady on the prospect of the exemplary behavior of her other children. This happy parent was blessed with numerous religious offspring! **It has given me great joy to find some of your children walking in the truth, just as the Father commanded us.** Possibly the lady's sons traveled abroad, either for accomplishment and acquaintance with the world, or on account of their own business or the common affairs of the family, and in their travels might have come to Ephesus, where the apostle was now supposed to reside, and might have there happily conversed with him. See how good it is to be trained up in early religion! Though religion is not to be founded upon education, yet education may be, and often is, blessed and is a way to fortify youth against irreligious infection. Hence too, let young travelers learn to carry their religion along with them, and not either leave it at home or learn the ill customs of the countries where they travel. It may be observed also that sometimes being chosen runs in a direct line; here is a **chosen lady** and her chosen **children**. Children may be loved for their parents' sake; but both are loved by virtue of free **grace**. From the apostle's joy in this we may observe that it is pleasant to see children treading in good parents' steps; and those who see this may well congratulate their parents on it, and they may both excite their thankfulness to God for so great a blessing and enlarge their comfort in it.

How happy a lady this was who had brought forth so many children for heaven and for God! And how great a joy must it be to her ladyship to hear so good an account of them from so good a judge! And we may further see that it is joyful to good old ministers, and accordingly to other good old disciples, to see a hopeful rising generation who may serve God and support religion in the world when they are dead and gone. We see here also the rule of true walking—as the Father commanded us. Our walk is true, our converse right, when it is managed by the Word of God.

5-6. And now, dear lady, I am not writing you a new command but one we have had from the beginning. I ask that we love one another. And this is love: that we walk in obedience to his commands. As you have heard from the beginning, his command is that you walk in love.

We come now more into the design and substance of the letter.

The Apostle's Request

Dear lady . . . I ask. Considering what it is that John requests, the way of address is very remarkable. It is not any particular gift or bounty to himself, but common duty and observance of divine command. Here he might command or charge, but harsher methods are worse than needless where milder ones will prevail; and the apostolic spirit is, of all others, the most tender and endearing. Whether out of deference to her ladyship or out of apostolic meekness or both, he condescends to beseech. We may suppose him to be speaking as another apostle does to a certain master to whom he writes, "Therefore, although in Christ I could be bold [according to the power with which Christ has entrusted me] and order you to do what you ought to do, yet I appeal to you on the basis of love" (Philemon 8-9). Love will avail where authority will not; and we may often see that the more authority is urged, the more it is slighted. The apostolic minister will love and appeal to his friends to do their duty.

What He Requests

What the apostle requests of the chosen lady and her children is Christian sacred love—**that we love one another** (verse 5). Those who are eminent in any Christian virtue still have room to grow in it. "Now about brotherly love we do not need to write to you, for you yourselves have been taught by God to love each other. And in fact, you do love all the brothers [and sisters] throughout Macedonia. Yet we urge you, brothers [and sisters], to do so more and more" (1 Thessalonians 4:9-10).

1. This love is recommended, first of all, as an obligation; it is a **com-**

mand. Divine commands should sway our mind and heart. Second, it is urged from the antiquity of the obligation; it is **not . . . a new command but one we have had from the beginning** (verse 5). This command of mutual Christian love may be said to be a **new** one in that it had been newly enacted and sanctioned by the Lord Christ; yet, as far as its essence is concerned (that is, mutual holy love), it is as old as natural, Jewish, or Christian religion. This **command** must go with Christianity everywhere; Christ's disciples must **love one another**.

2. Then this love is illustrated by its fruitful nature: **And this is love: that we walk in obedience to his commands** (verse 6). The test of our love to God is our obedience to him. It is also love to ourselves, to our own souls, when we walk in obedience to divine commands. "In keeping them there is great reward" (Psalm 19:11). Love to one another means urging each other to walk in holiness; this is the evidence of our sincere, mutual Christian love—that we walk after God's commands in all things. There can be mutual love that is not religious and Christian, but we know ours to be so by our observing all other commands besides that of mutual love. Universal obedience is the proof of the goodness and sincerity of Christian virtues; and those who aim at all Christian obedience will be sure to attend to Christian love. This is a fundamental duty in the Gospel charter: **this is love: that we walk in . . . obedience** (verse 6). Foreseeing the decay of this love, as well as other apostasy, perhaps made the apostle inculcate this duty and this prime command all the more frequently and earnestly.

The Bad News

7-9. Many deceivers, who do not acknowledge Jesus Christ as coming in the flesh, have gone out into the world. Any such person is the deceiver and the antichrist. Watch out that you do not lose what you have worked for, but that you may be rewarded fully. Anyone who runs ahead and does not continue in the teaching of Christ does not have God; whoever continues in the teaching has both the Father and the Son.

In the principal part of this letter we find, first of all, bad news communicated to the lady—namely, that seducers are about. Many deceivers, who do not acknowledge Jesus Christ as coming in the flesh, have gone out into the world (verse 7). This report is introduced in order to give a reason for the earlier exhortation: "You need to maintain your love, for there are destroyers of it in the world. Those who subvert the faith destroy this love. Secure your walk according to God's commands; this will establish you. Your stability is likely to be tried, for **many deceivers . . . have gone out into the world.**" Sad and saddening news must at times be communicated to our Christian friends; we should not love to make them sorry, but to forewarn is the way to forearm them against their trials.

1. Here is the description of the deceiver and his deceit: he does **not acknowledge Jesus Christ as coming in the flesh** (verse 7). He brings some error or other concerning the person of the Lord Jesus; either he does not confess that Jesus Christ is the same person, or that Jesus of Nazareth was the Christ or the anointed Son of God, the Messiah, promised from of old for the redemption of Israel, or that the promised Messiah and Redeemer has come in the flesh, into our world and into our nature. Such a person claims that Christ's coming is still to be expected. It is indeed strange that after our being given so much evidence, anyone should deny that the Lord Jesus is the Son of God and the Saviour of the world!

2. Here is the aggravation of the case: such a person is **the deceiver and the antichrist** (verse 7). He deludes souls and undermines the glory and kingdom of the Lord Christ. He must be an impostor, a willful **deceiver**, in view of all the light that has been given and all the evidence that Christ has manifested concerning himself and the attestation that God has given concerning his Son. Such a person is a willful opponent of the Lord Christ's person, honor, and interest, and as such he will be reckoned with when the Lord Christ comes again. Let us not think it strange that there are deceivers and opponents of the Lord Christ's name and dignity now, for there were such people in the past, even in the apostles' times.

The Apostle's Advice

Second, we find the counsel given to this chosen household concerning these deceivers. Care and caution are needed: **Watch out** (verse 8). The more delusions and deceits abound, the more watchful the disciples must be. Delusions may so prevail that even the chosen people may be endangered by them. Two things they must beware of:

1. They must **not lose what [they] have worked for** (verse 8), what they

have done or what they have gained. It is a pity that any religious labor should
be in vain; some begin well, but in the end lose all their labor. The hopeful gentleman who had kept the commands of the second tablet from his youth up
lost all rather than have less love to the world and more love to Christ. Those
who profess the name of Christ should take care not to lose what they have
gained. Many have not only gained a fair reputation for religion, but much
light therein, much conviction of the evil of sin, the vanity of the world, the
excellency of religion, and the power of God's Word. They have even "tasted
. . . the powers of the coming age" (Hebrews 6:5) and the gifts of the Holy
Spirit; yet in the end they lose everything. "You were running a good race.
Who cut in on you and kept you from obeying the truth?" (Galatians 5:7). It
is sad when fair and splendid attainments in Christ's school are lost in the end.

2. They most not lose their reward, no part of that honor or praise or
glory that they once stood to gain. **That you may be rewarded fully** (verse
8). John is saying in effect, "Seek to secure as full a reward as will be given
to any in the church of God. If there are degrees of glory, lose none of that
grace (that light or love or peace) that is to prepare you for the higher ele-
vation in glory."

"Hold on to what you have [in faith and hope and a good conscience],
so that no one will take your crown," so that you lose neither it nor any
jewel out of it (Revelation 3:11). The way to attain the full reward is to
remain true to Christ and constant in religion to the end.

The Reason for This Advice

The reason for the apostle's counsel, and of the care and caution they
should maintain about themselves, is twofold:

1. The danger and evil of departure from gospel light and revelation,
which is in effect and reality a departure from God himself. **Anyone who
runs ahead and does not continue in the teaching of Christ does not
have God** (verse 9). It is the teaching of Christ that is appointed to guide us
to God; it is that by which God draws souls to salvation and to himself.
Those who revolt against this, revolt against God.

2. The advantage and happiness of firm adherence to Christian truth is
that it unites us to Christ (the object, or subject matter, of that truth). Thus
it unites us also to the Father, for they are one. **Whoever continues**, being

rooted and grounded **in the teaching has both the Father and the Son** (verse 9). By the teaching of Christ we are enlightened in the knowledge of the Father and the Son; by it we are sanctified for the Father and the Son. Thereupon we are enriched with holy love to the Father and the Son, and thereby we are prepared for the endless enjoyment of the Father and the Son. "You are already clean because of the word I have spoken to you" (John 15:3). This purity makes us fit for heaven. Just as the great God has set his seal on the teaching of Christ, so he puts a value on it. We must retain that holy teaching in faith and love if we hope or desire to arrive at blessed communion with the Father and the Son.

How the Deceivers Should Be Treated

10-11. If anyone comes to you and does not bring this teaching, do not take him into your house or welcome him. Anyone who welcomes him shares in his wicked work.

Due warning having been given concerning seducers, the apostle now gives direction concerning their treatment. They are not to be entertained as the ministers of Christ. The Lord Christ will distinguish them from such, and he wants his disciples to do the same. The direction is negative:

1. "Do not support them." **If anyone comes to you and does not bring this teaching** (concerning Christ as the Son of God, the Messiah who is anointed by God for our redemption and salvation), **do not take him into your house** (verse 10). Possibly the lady was like Gaius, of whom we read in the next letter, a generous housekeeper and hospitable entertainer of traveling ministers and Christians. These deceivers might possibly expect the same reception as others, or as the best who came there (spiritually blind people are often that bold), but the apostle does not allow it. "Do not welcome them into your family." Doubtless such people may legitimately be relieved in their pressing necessities, but not encouraged for bad service. Those who deny the faith are destroyers of souls; and it is supposed that even gentle ladies should have a good understanding in religious matters.

2. "Do not bless their enterprises **or welcome him.** Do not give their service your prayers and good wishes." Bad work should not be consecrated or recommended to God for a blessing. God will never be a patron of falsehood, seduction, and sin. We ought to bid Godspeed to evangelical

ministering; but regarding the propagation of fatal error, if we cannot prevent it, we must not countenance it.

The Reason for This Prohibition

The reason the apostle forbids the support and patronage of the deceiver is that **anyone who welcomes him shares in his wicked work** (verse 11). Favor and affection partake of the sin; we may carelessly share in the iniquities of others. How sound in judgment and caution the Christian should be! There are many ways of sharing the guilt of other people's transgressions; it may be done by culpable silence, indolence, unconcernedness, private contribution, public countenance and assistance, inward approval, or open defense. May the Lord pardon our guilt for other people's sins!

12-13. I have much to write to you, but I do not want to use paper and ink. Instead, I hope to visit you and talk with you face to face, so that our joy may be complete. The children of your chosen sister send their greetings.

The apostle concludes this letter, first, by adjourning many things until he meets them personally (verse 12). He supposes that some things are better spoken than written. The use of pen and ink may be a mercy and a pleasure; but personal contact may be more so. The apostle was not yet too old for travel, nor consequently for traveling service. The communion of saints should be maintained by all methods, and their communion should produce mutual joy. Excellent ministers may have their joy advanced by their Christian friends. "That you and I may be mutually encouraged by each other's faith" (Romans 1:12).

Second, he presents the **greetings** of some near relatives of this lady (verse 13). Grace was abundant toward this family; here are two **chosen** sisters, and probably their chosen **children**. How they will admire this grace in heaven! The apostle condescends to insert the nieces' dutiful greetings to their aunt. Such greetings from younger relatives are to be cherished. Doubtless the apostle was readily available and would accept all friendly and pious overtures and was ready to enhance the good lady's joy in her nieces as well as in her children. May there be many such gracious ladies rejoicing in their gracious descendants and other relatives!

3 John
by Matthew Henry

3 John

Christian communion is exerted and cherished by letters. Christians are to be commended in the practical proof of their professed subjection to the Gospel of Christ. The animating and countenancing of generous and public-spirited people is doing good to many. To this end, the apostle sends this encouraging letter to his friend Gaius, in which also he complains of the quite opposite spirit and practice of a certain minister and confirms the good report concerning another who is more worthy to be imitated.

The apostle congratulates Gaius on the prosperity of his soul (1-2)
and on the fame he had among good Christians (3-4)
and on his charity and hospitality to Christ's servants (5-8).
He complains of contemptuous treatment by an ambitious Diotrephes (9-10).
He commends the imitation of good (11).
He recommends Demetrius (12)
and hopes to visit Gaul shortly (13-14).

1-2. The elder, To my dear friend Gaius, whom I love in the truth. Dear friend, I pray that you may enjoy good health and that all may go well with you, even as your soul is getting along well.

The Sacred Penman Who Writes and Sends the Letter

He is not, indeed, named here but is given a more general description—**the elder**. He is elder by years and by office; honor and deference are due to both. Some people have questioned whether this is John the apostle or not, but his style and spirit seem to shine in it. Those who are loved by Christ will love the brothers for his sake. Gaius could not question from whom the letter came. The apostle might have used many more illustrious descriptions of himself, but it does not become Christ's ministers to put forward pompous titles. He almost levels himself with the more ordinary pastors of the church when he simply calls himself **the elder**. Or possibly most of the extraordinary ministers, the apostles, were now dead, and this holy survivor would countenance the continued standing ministry by assuming the more common title, **the elder**. "To the elders among you, I appeal as a fellow elder" (1 Peter 5:1).

The Person Greeted and Honored by the Letter

The previous letter was directed to a "chosen lady," this to a chosen gentleman. Such people are worthy of esteem and value. He is designated, first, by his name, **Gaius**. We read of several of that name, particularly of one whom the apostle Paul baptized at Corinth, who possibly was also the apostle's host and kind entertainer there (Romans 16:23). If this is not the same man here, it is his brother in name, state, and disposition. He is then designated by the kind expressions of the apostle to him—**my dear friend** and **whom I love in the truth**. Love expressed has the habit of kindling love. Here seems to be either the sincerity of the apostle's love or the religion of it: the sincerity of it—**whom I love in the truth**, "whom I truly cordially love"; the religion of it—**whom I love in the truth**, for the truth's sake, as abiding and walking in **the truth** as it is in Jesus. To love our friends for the truth's sake is true love, gospel-love.

The Greeting

The greeting contains a prayer introduced by an affectionate appellation—My dear friend, one who is dear in Christ. The minister who wants to gain love must show it himself.

1. Here is the apostle's good opinion of his friend, that his **soul** was **getting along well** (verse 2). There is such a thing as soul-prosperity—the greatest blessing on this side of heaven. This supposes regeneration and an inward fund of spiritual life; while this stock is increasing and spiritual treasures are advancing, the soul is well on its way to the kingdom of glory.

2. Here also is his good wish for his friend, that his body **may enjoy good health** as well as his **soul**. Grace and health are two rich companions; grace will improve health, which will employ grace. It frequently falls out that a rich soul is lodged in a crazy body; grace must be exercised in submission to such a dispensation. But we may wish and pray that those who have prosperous souls may have healthy bodies too; their grace will then shine in a larger sphere of activity.

3-8. It gave me great joy to have some brothers come and tell about your faithfulness to the truth and how you continue to walk in the truth. I have no greater joy than to hear that my children are walking in the truth. Dear friend, you are faithful in what you are doing for the brothers, even though they are strangers to you. They have told the church about your love. You will do well to send them on their way in a manner worthy of God. It was for the sake of the Name that they went out, receiving no help from the pagans. We ought therefore to show hospitality to such men so that we may work together for the truth.

In these verses we have, first, the good report that the apostle had received concerning this friend of his: **some brothers** came and told **about your faithfulness to the truth** (verse 3); **they have told the church about your love** (verse 6). In this we may see:

1. The testimony or thing testified concerning the sincerity of his religion and devotion to God; this was revealed by his love, which included his love to the brothers, kindness to the poor, hospitality to Christian strangers, and a readiness to accommodate them for the service of the Gospel. Faith expresses itself through love (see Galatians 5:6); it gives a luster in and by the offices of love and induces others to commend its integrity.

2. The witnesses or **brothers** that came from Gaius **told**. A good report is due from those who have received good; though "a good name" is but a small reward for costly service, yet it "is better than fine perfume" (Ecclesiastes 7:1) and will not be refused by the honorable and the religious.

3. The audience, or judicatory, before which the report and testimony were given—**the church** (verse 6). This seems to be the church at which the

apostle was now living; what church it was, we are not sure. What occasion they had thus to testify concerning Gaius' **faithfulness** and **love** before **the church** (verses 3, 6) we cannot tell. Possibly the mouth spoke "out of the overflow of the heart" (Matthew 12:34); they could not but tell of what they had found and felt. Possibly they wanted to engage the church's prayer for the continued life and usefulness of such a patron, that he might enjoy good health and that all might go well with him.

Second, we have the report that the apostle himself gives of him, introduced by an endearing appellation again: **Dear friend, you are faithful in what you are doing for the brothers, even though they are strangers to you** (verse 5).

1. He was hospitable to **the brothers**, even to **strangers**. It was enough for Gaius that they belonged to Christ. He was good to **the brothers** of the same church as himself and to those who came from far away; all of the family of believers were welcome to him.

2. He seems to have been of a catholic spirit; he could overlook the petty differences among serious Christians and be communicative to all who bore the image and did the work of Christ.

3. He was conscientious in what he did: **you are faithful in what you are doing**—"you do it as a faithful servant, and you may expect a reward from the Lord Christ." Such faithful souls can hear their own praises without being puffed up; the commendation of what is good in us is designed not for our pride, but to get us to continue in it, and we should accordingly make the best of it.

Third, we see the apostle's joy in the good report itself and in the good ground of it: **It gave me great joy to have some brothers come and tell . . .** (verse 3); **I have no greater joy than to hear that my children are walking in the truth**, in what the Christian religion teaches (verse 4). The best evidence for our having **the truth** is our **walking in the truth**. Good people will greatly rejoice when other people's souls are getting along well; they are glad to hear of the grace and goodness of others. "They praised God because of me" (Galatians 1:24). Love does not envy but rejoices in the good name of other folks. As it is joy to good parents, it will be joy to good ministers to see their children manifest truth in their religion and so adorn their profession.

Fourth, we see the direction the apostle gives his friend concerning further treatment of the brothers who were with him: **You will do well to send them** on their way **in a manner worthy of God** (verse 6). It seems to have been customary in those days of love to look after or even accompany traveling ministers and Christians, at least for part of their way (see 1 Corinthians 16:6). It is a kindness to a stranger to be guided in his way, and a pleasure to travelers to meet with suitable company. This is a work that may be done **in a manner worthy of God**—suitable to the deference and relation we bear to God. Christians should consider not only what they *must* do, but what they *may* do—what they may most honorably and laudably do; "the noble man makes noble plans," generous ones (Isaiah 32:8). Christians should do even the common actions of life and of goodwill **in a manner worthy of God**, as serving God in those actions and intending his glory.

Fifth, we have the reasons of this directed conduct:

1. **It was for the sake of the Name that they went out, receiving no help from the pagans** (verse 7). So it appears that these were ministerial brothers who went out to preach the Gospel and propagate Christianity. Possibly they were sent out by the apostle himself. They **went out** to convert **the pagans**. This was excellent service; **they went out** for God and **for the sake of the Name**. This is the minister's highest end and should be his principal spring and motive, to gather and to build up a people **for the sake of the Name**. Also, **they went out** to carry a free Gospel with them, **receiving no help from the pagans**, and thus evidently being supported by other believers. These were worthy of a double honor. There are those who are not called to preach the Gospel themselves and who yet contribute much to its progress. The Gospel should be offered without charge to those to whom it is first preached; those who do not know it cannot be expected to value it. Churches and Christian patriots ought to concur to support the propagation of holy religion in pagan countries; public-spirited Christians should lend their support in whatever way they are able. Those who communicate Christ's Gospel freely should be assisted by those who communicate from their purses.

2. **We ought therefore to show hospitality to such men so that we may work together for the truth** (verse 8)—that is, for true religion. The religion of Christ is the true religion. It has been attested by God; those who are true in it and true to it will earnestly desire and pray for and contribute to its propagation in the world. The truth may be befriended and assisted in many ways; those who cannot themselves proclaim it may still receive, accompany, help, and countenance those who do.

9-11. I wrote to the church, but Diotrephes, who loves to be first, will

have nothing to do with us. So if I come, I will call attention to what he is doing, gossiping maliciously about us. Not satisfied with that, he refuses to welcome the brothers. He also stops those who want to do so and puts them out of the church. Dear friend, do not imitate what is evil but what is good. Anyone who does what is good is from God. Anyone who does what is evil has not seen God.

Here is a very different example and character—an officer, a minister in the church, who was less generous, catholic, and communicative than the private Christians. Ministers may sometimes be outshone, outdone.

In reference to this minister, we see, first, his name—a Gentile name—Diotrephes, accompanied by an unchristian spirit.

Second, we see his temper and spirit as full of pride and ambition, for he loves to be first. This ferment is an ill, unbecoming character of Christ's ministers—to love to be first, to seek presidency and precedency in the church of God.

Third, we see his contempt of the apostle's authority, letter, and friends:

1. John's authority: what he is doing was contrary to instructions, gossiping maliciously about us (verse 10). It was strange that the contempt should be so great. But ambition will breed malice against those who oppose it. Malice and ill will in the heart will likely vent itself by the lips. The heart and mouth are both to be watched.

2. John's letter: I wrote to the church (verse 9) recommending such and such brothers, but Diotrephes . . . will have nothing to do with us. That is, "He does not admit our letter and what we say in it." This seems to be the church of which Gaius was a member. A gospel-proclaiming church is the sort of society to which a letter may be written and communicated. Gospel-churches may well expect and be allowed credentials concerning the strangers who desire to be admitted among them. The apostle seems to write by and with these brothers. But to an ambitious, aspiring spirit, apostolic authority signifies but little.

3. John's friends, the brothers he recommended: He refuses to welcome the brothers. He also stops those who want to do so and puts them out of the church (verse 10). There might be some differences or different customs between, for example, Jewish and Gentile Christians. Pastors should seriously consider what differences are tolerable. The pastor is not at absolute liberty, nor is he to lord it over God's heritage. It is bad to do no good ourselves, but it is worse to hinder those who want to do it. Church power and church censures are often abused. Many people are thrown out

of the church who should be received there with satisfaction and welcome. Woe to those who cast out brothers whom the Lord Christ will take into his own communion and kingdom!

4. The apostle's warning to this proud tyrant: **So, if I come, I will call attention to what he is doing** (verse 10). This seems to suggest apostolic authority. But the apostle seems not to refer to an episcopal court to which Diotrephes must be summoned, but will rather come to take cognizance of this affair in the church to which it belongs.

In addition to Diotrephes' character, there is advice about it and dissuasion from copying such a pattern, and indeed any evil at all: **Dear friend, do not imitate what is evil but what is good** (verse 11). That is, "Do not imitate such unchristian, pernicious evil, but pursue the contrary good, in wisdom, purity, peace, and love." Caution and counsel are not unnecessary for those who are already good. The cautions and counsels that are most likely to be accepted are those that are seasoned with love. **Dear friend, do not imitate what is evil.** A reason is given for this caution and counsel:

For the counsel: **Imitate . . . what is good,** for **anyone who does what is good** (who naturally and genuinely does good because he delights in it) **is from God;** he is born of God. The practice of goodness is the evidence of our filial and happy relation to God.

For the caution: **Do not imitate what is evil. . . . Anyone who does what is evil** (who with bent of mind pursues it) **has not seen God;** he is not aware of God's holy nature and will. Evil-workers vainly pretend or boast an acquaintance with God.

12-14. **Demetrius is well spoken of by everyone—and even by the truth itself. We also speak well of him, and you know that our testimony is true. I have much to write you, but I do not want to do so with pen and ink. I hope to see you soon, and we will talk face to face. Peace to you. The friends here send their greetings. Greet the friends there by name.**

The Character of Another Person

Demetrius is not much known otherwise, but here his name will live. A name in the Gospel, a fame in the churches, is better than that of sons and daughters. His character was his commendation.

1. His commendation was general: **Demetrius is well spoken of by**

everyone (verse 12). Few are well spoken of by all, and sometimes it is ill to be so. But universal integrity and goodness are the way to (and sometimes obtain) universal applause.

2. His commendation was deserved and well founded: **and even by the truth itself** (verse 12). Some people are well spoken of, but not by the truth. Happy are those whose spirit and conduct recommend them before God and before men and women.

3. His commendation was confirmed by the apostle's and his friends' testimony: **We also speak well of him** (verse 12). The apostle then appeals to Gaius' own knowledge: **And you** (that is, you and your friends) **know that our testimony is true.** Probably this Demetrius was known to the church where the apostle now resided and to the church where Gaius then was. It is good to be known for good. We must be ready to bear our testimony to those who are good; this is a debt to virtue and goodness. It is well for those who are commended when those who commend them can appeal to the consciences of those who know them most.

The Conclusion of the Letter

1. Some things were left until they would meet personally: **I have much to write you, but I do not want to do so with pen and ink. I hope to see you soon, and we will talk face to face** (verses 13-14). Many things may be more appropriately communicated directly than by letter. A little personal talk may spare the time, trouble, and cost of many letters, and good Christians may well be glad to see one another.

2. Observe the blessing: **Peace to you.** That is, "May all happiness be with you." Those who are good and happy themselves wish others to be so as well.

3. A public greeting is sent to Gaius: **The friends here send their greetings.** A friend in the propagation of religion deserves a common remembrance, and these pious people show their friendship to religion as well as to Gaius.

4. The apostle particularly greets the Christians in Gaius' church or vicinity: **Greet the friends there by name.** I doubt if there were very many to be greeted personally, but we must learn humility as well as love. The lowest in the church of Christ should be greeted. And believers do well to greet one another on earth since they hope to live together in heaven. The apostle who had reclined next to Jesus held Christ's friends in his heart.